Reteaching and Practice
Workbook

Grade 3

Scott Foresman·Addison Wesley

enVisionMATH®
Common Core

PEARSON

Glenview, Illinois • Boston, Massachusetts • Chandler, Arizona • Upper Saddle River, New Jersey

ISBN-13: 978-0-328-81075-8

ISBN-10: 0-328-81075-4

1 2 3 4 5 6 7 8 9 10 V0N4 17 16 15 14 13

Contents

Name _____

Reteaching
1-1

Representing Numbers

Here are different ways to show 365.

place-value blocks:

expanded form: 300 + 60 + 5

standard form: 365

word form: three hundred sixty-five

Write each number in standard form.

1. _____

2. _____

3. 400 + 40 + 8 _____

4. seven hundred fifty-five _____

Write each number in expanded form.

5. 240 _____

6. 381 _____

7. Write a 3-digit number with a 7 in the hundreds place and a 6 in the ones place. _____

8. **Reason** Jason put the digits 7, 2, and 6 in order to make the greatest possible number. What is Jason's number? _____

Name _____

Representing Numbers

Write each number in standard form.

1.

_____

2.

_____

3. 900 + 40 + 7

_____

4. 600 + 70 + 1

_____

Write each number in expanded form.

5. 793

_____

6. 308

_____

Write the place of the underlined digit. Then write its value.

7. <u>3</u>42

_____

8. <u>7</u>95

_____

9. 3<u>9</u>8

_____

10. Communicate An arena can seat nine hundred forty-eight people.
How is that number written in standard form? Explain.

_____

_____

11. Which is the word form of 840?

    A eight hundred forty

    B eight thousand, forty

    C eight hundred four

    D eight thousand, four hundred

Understanding Number Lines

The distance on a number line between any whole number and the next whole number is exactly the same.

You can make the numbers closer together or farther apart. The numbers in the number line below are closer together than the numbers in the number line above.

Both number lines show the same numbers.

Write the value of *A* and *B* for each number line.

1.

_____

2.

_____

3. Reason Which letter on this number line has the greater value: *A* or *B*? Explain your answer.

_____

_____

_____

Understanding Number Lines

Write the value of *A*, *B*, and *C* on each number line.

1.

0   1   2   *A*   4   5   *B*   7   *C*   9   10

2.

14   *A*   16   17   18   *B*   20   *C*   22

3.

A   26   27   28   29   *B*   31   32   33   34   *C*

4. Texas became a state in 1845. Draw a point to show where 1845 is on the number line.

1800 1810 1820 1830 1840 1850 1860 1870 1880 1890 1900

5. Critique Reasoning Lara said that point *D* has a value of 38. Is her statement reasonable? Explain your answer.

D

0   5   10   15   20   25   30   35   40   45   50

_____

_____

6. Which letter represents 57 on this number line?

50   *E*   *F*   *G*   *H*   60

A *E*   **B** *F*   **C** *G*   **D** *H*

Counting on the Number Line

A number line can be used to show a pattern. No matter what the pattern is, any whole number and the next whole number are always the same distance apart.

The pattern is to add 4 to the previous number.

Write the missing numbers on each number line.

1.

2.

3.

4. Use Structure Make a number line from 0 to 60 counting by sixes.

Counting on the Number Line

Write the missing numbers for each number line.

1.

0   4   ☐   ☐   16   ☐   24   ☐   32   ☐   40

2.

10   ☐   22   ☐   34   ☐   46   ☐   58

3.

☐   24   ☐   40   ☐   ☐   64   72   ☐

Write the number that points *J* and *K* represent on each number line.

4.

30   J   K   120

_____

5.

20   J   K   120

_____

6. Communicate How can you find what each mark represents on a number line?

_____

_____

7. Which point on the number line represents 18?

0   A   B   27   36   45   C   63   72   D   90

A *A*   **B** *B*   **C** *C*   **D** *D*

Finding the Halfway Number

A halfway number is a number that is the same distance away from two other numbers. One number will be less than the halfway number. The other number will be greater than the halfway number.

What number is halfway between 0 and 10?

Try 5.

There are 5 numbers before 5: 0, 1, 2, 3, 4.
There are 5 numbers after 5: 6, 7, 8, 9, 10.

So, 5 is the halfway number between 0 and 10.

Find the number halfway between each pair of numbers.

1.   _____

2.   _____

3.   _____

4. Draw It Draw a number line from 70 to 80 numbered by ones. Place a dot at the halfway number.

Finding the Halfway Number

Find the number halfway between each pair of numbers.
You may draw number lines to help.

1. 30 and 40

_____

2. 60 and 70

_____

3. 80 and 90

_____

4. 200 and 300

_____

5. 400 and 500

_____

6. 600 and 700

_____

7. 3,000 and 4,000

_____

8. 6,000 and 7,000

_____

9. 7,000 and 8,000

_____

Find the halfway number for each number line.

10.
20 21 22 23 24 25 26 27 28 29 30

_____

11.
100 110 120 130 140 150 160 170 180 190 200

_____

12. **Reason** Tony says that 4,400 is halfway between 4,000 and 5,000. Is he correct? Why or why not?

_____

_____

_____

_____

13. Which number is halfway between 2,000 and 3,000?

A 2,050

B 2,500

C 2,550

D 2,750

Rounding

You can use place value to round to the nearest ten or hundred.

Find the rounding place. If the digit to the right of the rounding place is 5, 6, 7, 8, or 9, then increase the digit in the rounding place by one. If the digit is less than 5, do not change the digit in the rounding place.

Round 17 to the nearest ten: 20

Explain. 7 is in the ones place. Round to the next greater ten.

Round 153 to the nearest ten. 150

Explain. Because 3 is in the ones place and 3 is less than 5, the digit in the tens place does not change.

Round 575 to the nearest hundred. 600

Explain. Because the 7 in the tens place is 5 or greater, round to the next greater hundred.

1. Round 63 to the nearest ten: _____

   Explain. _____

Round each number to the nearest ten.

2. 58   3. 71   4. 927   5. 195

_____   _____   _____   _____

Round each number to the nearest hundred.

6. 577   7. 820   8. 350   9. 875

_____   _____   _____   _____

10. **Reasonableness** If you live 71 miles from a river, does it make sense to say you live about 80 miles from the river? Explain.

_____

Rounding

Round to the nearest ten.

1. 37   **2.** 93   **3.** 78   **4.** 82   **5.** 24

_____   _____   _____   _____   _____

6. 426   **7.** 329   **8.** 815   **9.** 163   **10.** 896

_____   _____   _____   _____   _____

Round to the nearest hundred.

11. 395   **12.** 638   **13.** 782   **14.** 246   **15.** 453

_____   _____   _____   _____   _____

16. 529   **17.** 877   **18.** 634   **19.** 329   **20.** 587

_____   _____   _____   _____   _____

21. Critique Reasoning Tyrell says 753 rounds to 800. Sara says 753 rounds to 750. Who is correct? Explain.

_____

_____

22. Communicate How would you use a number line to round 148 to the nearest ten? Explain.

_____

_____

23. There are 254 counties in Texas. What is that number rounded to the nearest ten? What is that number rounded to the nearest hundred?

_____

24. Reason Which number does not round to 400?

    A 347   **B** 369   **C** 413   **D** 448

More Rounding

As with 2- and 3-digit numbers, you can use place value to round 4-digit numbers.

How do you round 4,627 to the nearest ten? nearest hundred?

To round a 4-digit number to the nearest ten, look at the digit in the *ones* place. If the ones digit is 5 or greater, then increase the tens digit by one. If the ones digit is less than 5, then do not change the tens digit.	To round a 4-digit number to the nearest hundred, look at the digit in the *tens* place. If the tens digit is 5 or greater, then increase the hundreds digit by one. If the tens digit is less than 5, then do not change the hundreds digit.
4,6**2**7	4,6**2**7
7 > 5, so 4,627 rounds to 4,630	2 < 5, so 4,627 rounds to 4,600

Remember to change the digits in the place or places less than the rounding place to 0.

Round to the nearest ten.

1. 752   **2.** 426   **3.** 3,421   **4.** 5,718   **5.** 8,356

_____   _____   _____   _____   _____

Round to the nearest hundred.

6. 376   **7.** 629   **8.** 6,742   **9.** 7,095   **10.** 8,976

_____   _____   _____   _____   _____

11. Writing to Explain How do you round 6,318 to the nearest hundred? Give the rounded number.

_____

_____

_____

_____

_____

Name _____

More Rounding

Round to the nearest ten.

1. 295 _____   2. 981 _____

3. 1,875 _____   4. 2,743 _____

5. 1,209 _____   6. 5,097 _____

7. 7,805 _____   8. 3,715 _____

9. 4,610 _____   10. 6,724 _____

Round to the nearest hundred.

11. 2,382 _____   12. 3,726 _____

13. 5,067 _____   14. 6,348 _____

15. 7,957 _____   16. 1,738 _____

17. 7,451 _____   18. 9,682 _____

19. 8,046 _____   20. 9,974 _____

Use the digits 3, 7, 1, and 5 to write a number that rounds to each of the following.

21. 1,700   22. 3,500   23. 1,600   24. 7,400

_____   _____   _____   _____

25. **Reason** Alice said that 3,642 rounds to 3,600. Ned said it rounds to 3,640. Who is correct?

_____

_____

_____

26. Which number rounds to 3,800 when you round it to the nearest hundred?

A 3,736

B 3,748

C 3,829

D 3,853

P 1·6

Problem Solving: Make an Organized List

Todd has given Maclan the information below to guess one or more 3-digit numbers that fit the clues.

- The ones digit is odd.

- The tens digit is greater than 8.

- The hundreds digit is less than 2.

Use the clues for each digit to make an organized list.

The ones digit is odd.	The tens digit is greater than 8.	The hundreds digit is less than 2.
The odd numbers are 1, 3, 5, 7, and 9.	The only digit greater than 8 is 9. The tens digit is 9.	The digit in the greatest place of a whole number cannot be 0. The hundreds digit is 1.

So, the numbers that fit the clues are 191, 193, 195, 197, and 199.

Make an organized list to solve.

1. Barbara, Lisa, and Maria are having their picture taken for the yearbook. List the ways that they can stand in a straight line for the picture. You can use their initials.

   _____

   _____

2. List all the 3-digit numbers that fit these clues.

   - The hundreds digit is greater than 7.
   - The tens digit is less than 2.
   - The ones digit is the same as the hundreds digit.

   _____

   _____

3. **Reason** In how many ways can you make 10 cents using dimes, nickels, and pennies? List all the ways.

   _____

   _____

Problem Solving: Make an Organized List

Make an organized list to solve.

1. List all the 3-digit numbers that fit these clues.

   • The hundreds digit is less than 3.
   • The tens digit is less than 2.
   • The ones digit is greater than 7.

   _____

   _____

2. List all the 3-digit numbers that fit these clues.

   • The hundreds digit is greater than 7.
   • The tens is 1 more than the hundreds digit.
   • The ones digit is less than 2.

   _____

   _____

3. Jim and Sarah are running for class president. Cayla and Daniel are running for vice president. What combinations of president and vice president could there be?

   _____

   _____

4. List all the ways that you can arrange the letters A, B, and C.

   _____

   _____

   _____

5. **Persevere** What is this 3-digit number?

   • The hundreds digit is 4 greater than 3.
   • The tens digit is 1 more than the hundreds digit.
   • The ones digit is 3 less than the tens digit.

   _____

6. In how many ways can you make 30 cents using quarters, dimes, and nickels?

   A 4

   B 5

   C 6

   D 8

Addition Meaning and Properties

The Commutative (Order) Property

You can add numbers in any order, and the sum will be the same.

6 + 2 = 8   2 + 6 = 8

The Associative (Grouping) Property

You can group addends in any way, and the sum will be the same.

(3 + 4) + 1 = 8   3 + (4 + 1) = 8

The Identity (Zero) Property

The sum of any number and zero equals that same number.

0 + 4 = 4

Find each sum.

1. 3 + (2 + 4) = _____   **2.** (0 + 5) + 2 = _____

3. (8 + 3) + 4 = _____   **4.** 9 + 2 + 6 = _____

Write each missing number.

5. 3 + 4 = 4 + _____   **6.** _____ + 7 = 7

7. (2 + 3) + 4 = _____ + (3 + 4)   **8.** 9 + (2 + 7) = (9 + 2) + _____

9. Reason Does (4 + 5) + 2 = 9 + 2? Explain.

_____

_____

Addition Meaning and Properties

Write each missing number.

1. $7 + 2 = 2 + \blacksquare$

2. $3 + \blacksquare = 3$

3. $(2 + 4) + 5 = 2 + (\blacksquare + 5)$

_____

_____

_____

4. $3 + \blacksquare = 5 + 3$

5. $\blacksquare + 0 = 6$

6. $(5 + 3) + 9 = 8 + \blacksquare$

_____

_____

_____

7. Use Structure What property of addition is shown in the following number sentence? Explain.

$7 + (3 + 5) = (7 + 3) + 5$

_____

_____

8. Minnie has 6 country CDs and 5 rock CDs.
Amanda has 5 rock CDs and 6 country CDs.
Who has more CDs? Explain.

_____

_____

9. Show how the Commutative Property of Addition works using the numbers 2, 3, and 5.

_____

10. Critique Reasoning Jake says that adding 0 does not change a sum. Is he correct? Explain.

_____

_____

11. Which property of addition is shown by $5 + 2 = 2 + 5$?

   A Associative Property

   C Commutative Property

   B Distributive Property

   D Identity Property

Subtraction Meanings

Dawn received a total of 12 stars on Monday and Tuesday. She received 7 of the stars on Monday. How many stars did she receive on Tuesday?

You can draw a picture to find how many stars Dawn received on Tuesday.

First, draw 12 stars.

Next, put a line through the 7 stars that Dawn received Monday.

Count the number of stars that are not crossed off.
There are 5.
So, $12 - 7 = 5$.

You can add to check subtraction: $7 + 5 = 12$, so $12 - 7 = 5$.

Dawn received 5 stars on Tuesday.

Find each difference. Make a drawing to help you.

1. $13 - 4 =$ _____

2. $16 - 9 =$ _____

3. $15 - 7 =$ _____

4. $11 - 6 =$ _____

5. $12 - 8 =$ _____

6. $14 - 5 =$ _____

7. **Estimation** There are 21 players on the Titans baseball team. Only 9 players can play at any one time. About how many players are not playing? _____

8. An octagon has 8 sides. A pentagon has 5 sides. How many more sides does an octagon have than a pentagon? _____

Name _____

Subtraction Meanings

Write a number sentence for each situation. Solve.

1. Terrance has 14 CDs. Robyn has 9 CDs. How many more CDs does Terrance have than Robyn?

_____

2. How many more black stars are there than white stars?

_____

3. Arizona has 15 counties. Connecticut has 8 counties. How many more counties does Arizona have than Connecticut?

_____

4. A baseball hat costs $12. Nancy has a coupon for $4 off. How much money will Nancy spend on the baseball hat?

_____

5. Carrie invited 13 girls to a party. Five of the girls have already arrived. How many girls have yet to arrive? Draw a picture to show the problem.

_____

6. **Use Structure** Write the fact family for 3, 9, and 12.

_____

_____

_____

7. LaToya has 12 postcards and 4 photographs on a bulletin board. How many more postcards does LaToya have than photographs?

   A 7   **B** 8   **C** 9   **D** 16

Name _____

Using Mental Math to Add

You can break apart numbers to make them easier to add mentally.

Add 31 + 45 by breaking apart numbers.

Break the numbers into tens and ones.

	tens	ones
31 =	30	+ 1
45 =	40	+ 5

Add the tens: 30 + 40 = 70.

Add the ones: 1 + 5 = 6.

Add the sums: 70 + 6 = 76.

So, 31 + 45 = 76.

Add 26 + 17 by breaking apart numbers to make a ten.

Use a number that adds with the 6 in 26 to make a 10. Since 6 + 4 = 10, use 4.

Think: 17 = 4 + 13.

Add 26 + 4 = 30.

Add 30 + 13 = 43.

So, 26 + 17 = 43.

Find each sum using mental math.

1. 24 + 71 = _____   **2.** 36 + 43 = _____   **3.** 54 + 23 = _____

4. 25 + 49 = _____   **5.** 37 + 56 = _____   **6.** 77 + 13 = _____

7. Communicate To add 32 + 56, Juanita first added 30 + 50.
What two steps does she still need to do to find the sum?
What is Juanita's sum?

_____

_____

8. Reason How can Steve add 48 + 34 by making a ten?
What is the sum?

_____

_____

_____

R 2·3

Using Mental Math to Add

Use breaking apart to add mentally.

1. 53 + 34

34 = 30 + ☐

53 + ☐ = 83

83 + ☐ = 87

So, 53 + 34 = ☐

2. 42 + 29

29 = 20 + ☐

42 + ☐ = 62

☐ + 9 = 71

So, 42 + 29 = ☐

3. 47 + 41

41 = ☐ + 1

47 + ☐ = 87

☐ + 1 = 88

So, 47 + 41 = ☐

Make a ten to add mentally.

4. 27 + 24

24 = 3 + ☐

27 + ☐ = 30

☐ + 21 = 51

So, 27 + 24 = ☐

5. 54 + 19

19 = ☐ + 6

☐ + 6 = 60

60 + ☐ = 73

So, 54 + 19 = ☐

6. 38 + 27

27 = ☐ + 25

38 + ☐ = 40

40 + ☐ = 65

So, 38 + 27 = ☐

Find each sum using mental math.

7. 52 + 26

_____

8. 47 + 8

_____

9. 32 + 17

_____

10. 28 + 31

_____

11. 43 + 38

_____

12. 72 + 7

_____

13. 42 + 33

_____

14. 36 + 14

_____

15. Generalize Ashton broke apart a number into 30 + 7.
What number did he start with?

_____

16. What is the sum of 27 + 42 using mental math?

A 68   **B** 69   **C** 78   **D** 79

Using Mental Math to Subtract

You can change numbers to make subtraction problems easier.

There are two ways to subtract 42 − 28.

One way is to add 2 to 28.

$$\begin{array}{r} 42 \quad\;\; \to 42 \\ -\;28 + 2 \to 30 \\ \hline 12 \end{array}$$

Because you added 2 to 28, add 2 to the difference.

12 + 2 = 14

So, 42 − 28 = 14.

Another way is to add 2 to both 42 and 28.

$$\begin{array}{r} 42 + 2 \to 44 \\ -\;28 + 2 \to 30 \\ \hline 14 \end{array}$$

What you do to the bottom number, also do to the top number.

So, 42 − 28 = 14.

Find each difference using mental math.

1. 32 − 17 = _____ **2.** 51 − 46 = _____ **3.** 42 − 18 = _____

4. 36 − 19 = _____ **5.** 63 − 56 = _____ **6.** 78 − 16 = _____

7. 94 − 18 = _____ **8.** 55 − 33 = _____ **9.** 81 − 13 = _____

10. Model Rob had $60 when he went to the mall. He bought a DVD for $15. How much money does he have left? Write the number sentence you used to solve the problem.

_____

R 2•4

Using Mental Math to Subtract

Find each difference using mental math.

1. 38 − 14   **2.** 42 − 13   **3.** 55 − 12   **4.** 62 − 17

_____   _____   _____   _____

5. 72 − 19   **6.** 94 − 11   **7.** 32 − 15   **8.** 85 − 18

_____   _____   _____   _____

9. 43 − 16   **10.** 66 − 15   **11.** 53 − 19   **12.** 72 − 16

_____   _____   _____   _____

13. Reason Gillian started solving 88 − 29.
This is what she did.

$$88 - 29 = ?$$
$$88 - 30 = 58$$

What should Gillian do next?   _____

14. Communicate Tell how to find 81 − 16 using mental math.

_____

_____

_____

15. Tiffany will use a total of 63 tiles for her art project. She only
needs 17 more tiles. Use mental math to find how many tiles
she has already.

_____

16. To solve 35 − 19, Jack used 35 − 20. What did he do next?

A Added 1   **C** Subtracted 1

B Subtracted 9   **D** Added 9

Estimating Sums

The students at your school are saving cereal box tops.

136
box tops

152
box tops

About how many box tops have the students saved?

When you find about how many, you estimate.

Estimate by rounding each addend. Then add the rounded numbers.

Round to the nearest ten.	Round to the nearest hundred.
136 → 140	136 → 100
+ 152 → 150	+ 152 → 200
290	300
The students have saved about 290 box tops.	The students have saved about 300 box tops.

Round to the nearest ten to estimate each sum.

1. 42 + 98 = _____   **2.** 36 + 59 = _____   **3.** 288 + 475 = _____

Round to the nearest hundred to estimate each sum.

4. 378 + 136 = _____   **5.** 436 + 309 = _____   **6.** 76 + 487 = _____

7. Critique Reasoning Sun-Yi estimated 270 + 146 and got 300.
Is her estimate reasonable? Explain.

_____

_____

_____

Estimating Sums

Round to the nearest ten to estimate.

1. 58 + 43   **2.** 87 + 69   **3.** 37 + 141   **4.** 422 + 296

_____   _____   _____   _____

Round to the nearest hundred to estimate.

5. 536 + 393   **6.** 242 + 359   **7.** 713 + 82   **8.** 313 + 405

_____   _____   _____   _____

Use compatible numbers to estimate.

9. 83 + 34   **10.** 329 + 64   **11.** 212 + 347   **12.** 537 + 244

_____   _____   _____   _____

13. Reasonableness Miguel has 325 baseball cards and
272 football cards. He said that he has 597 cards
in all. Is his answer reasonable? Explain using estimation.

_____

_____

_____

_____

14. Write a Problem Natalie has 138 DVDs and 419 CDs. Write
a number sentence that you could use to estimate the sum of
the DVDs and CDs. Then find your estimated sum.

_____

15. Which of the following shows estimating 287 + 491 by using
compatible numbers?

A 100 + 500   **B** 300 + 400   **C** 280 + 400   **D** 280 + 500

Estimating Differences

Members of the Biology Club caught 288 butterflies and 136 grasshoppers in their nets. About how many more butterflies than grasshoppers did the club catch?

You can estimate by rounding. To round to a certain place, look at the digit to the right of that place. If the digit is 5 or greater, round up. If the digit is less than 5, round down.

Round to the nearest hundred.	**Round to the nearest ten.**
Look at the digits in the tens place.	Look at the digits in the ones place.

$$\begin{array}{rcl} 288 & \to & 300 \\ -\ 136 & \to & 100 \\ \hline & & 200 \end{array}$$

$$\begin{array}{rcl} 288 & \to & 290 \\ -\ 136 & \to & 140 \\ \hline & & 150 \end{array}$$

There were about 200 more butterflies than grasshoppers caught.

There were about 150 more butterflies than grasshoppers caught.

Estimate by rounding to the nearest hundred.

1. $\begin{array}{r} 442 \\ -\ 112 \\ \hline \end{array}$

2. $\begin{array}{r} 725 \\ -\ 278 \\ \hline \end{array}$

3. $\begin{array}{r} 363 \\ -\ 187 \\ \hline \end{array}$

Estimate by rounding to the nearest ten.

4. $68 - 42 = $ _____

5. $88 - 17 = $ _____

6. $231 - 109 = $ _____

7. **Critique Reasoning** Charlie estimated $293 - 44$ and got a difference of about 250. Is this a reasonable estimate? Explain.

_____

_____

_____

Estimating Differences

Round to the nearest hundred to estimate each difference.

1. 478 − 267

2. 236 − 119

3. 588 − 321

_____   _____   _____

Round to the nearest ten to estimate each difference.

4. 677 − 421

5. 296 − 97

6. 312 − 157

_____   _____   _____

Use compatible numbers to estimate each difference.

7. 84 − 36

8. 427 − 163

9. 609 − 243

_____   _____   _____

10. Critique Reasoning Fern rounded to the nearest ten to estimate
548 − 132. She subtracted 540 − 130 and got 410. Is Fern's
estimate correct? Explain.

_____

_____

11. On Friday, 537 people attended a play.
For Saturday's matinee, there were 812 people.
About how many more people attended
the play on Saturday than on Friday?   _____

12. A football team scored 529 points one season
and then 376 points the next. About how many
points less did the team score in the second
season? Round to the nearest ten.   _____

13. Waco, TX, has an elevation of 405 feet.
Dallas, TX, has an elevation of 463 feet.
About how many feet greater is Dallas's
elevation than Waco's elevation?

    A 470 − 400 = 70

    B 460 − 410 = 50

    C 450 + 400 = 850

    D 460 + 400 = 860

Problem Solving: Reasonableness

The island of Elba has an area of 86 square miles. The island of St. Helena has an area of 47 square miles. How many square miles larger is Elba than St. Helena?

You can subtract to find how many square miles larger Elba is than St. Helena. Use mental math or a hundred chart to subtract.

$86 - 47 = 39$

Make sure you answered the correct question.

The question asked how many square miles larger Elba is than St. Helena. The correct question was answered.

86 square miles in all	
47	?

Elba is 39 square miles larger than St. Helena.

Make sure that your answer is reasonable.

Since $47 + 39 = 86$, the answer is reasonable.

---

1. The JP Morgan Chase Tower in Houston has 75 stories. The Renaissance Tower in Dallas has 56 stories. How many more stories does the JP Morgan Chase Tower have than the Renaissance Tower?

75 stories in all	
56	

2. The Bulldogs scored 49 points in last week's game. This week, they scored 62 points. How many points did the Bulldogs score in all in the two games?

_____ points in all	
49	62

3. **Write a Problem** Write a problem about something you did that can be solved using addition or subtraction. Then solve the problem and check that your answer is reasonable.

_____

_____

_____

Name _____

Problem Solving:
Reasonableness

Solve. Then check that your answer is reasonable.

1. The Aggies scored 59 points in
    the first half and 56 points in the
    second half. How many points did
    the Aggies score altogether?

_____ points in all	
59	56

2. Ms. Rice is driving 92 miles to a
    meeting. After driving 54 miles, she
    stops to buy gasoline. How many
    more miles does she have left?

92 miles in all	
54	

3. There are 45 students going on a
    field trip. Of those students, 27 are
    from Mrs. Unser's class. The rest
    are from Mr. King's class. How
    many students are from Mr. King's
    class?

45 students in all	
27	

4. **Estimation** In the 2004 Summer
    Olympics, the United States won
    36 gold, 39 silver, and 27 bronze
    medals. About how many medals
    did the United States win?

_____ medals in all		
40	40	30

5. Christine is reading a short story
    that is 76 pages long. She just
    finished reading page 47. How
    many more pages does she have
    left to read?

76 pages in all	
47	

6. Wyoming has 23 counties.
    Wisconsin has 49 more counties
    than Wyoming. How many
    counties does Wisconsin have?

    A 26   **C** 72

    B 62   **D** 82

Adding with an Expanded Algorithm

Find 234 + 451.

You can use place-value blocks to show each number.	**Step 1** Break the problem into smaller problems.	**Step 2** Add the sums.

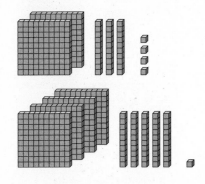

Step 1
Break the problem into smaller problems.

	H	T	O
234 =	200	30	4
451 =	400	50	1
Sums →	600	80	5

Step 2
Add the sums.

Hundreds ⟶ 600

Tens ⟶ 80

Ones ⟶ + 5
_____
234 + 451 = 685

---

1. 211 + 334

Hundreds	Tens	Ones	Total
200	10	1	_____
+ 300	+ 30	+ 4	_____
			+ _____

2. 516 + 140

Hundreds	Tens	Ones	Total
500	10	6	_____
+ 100	+ 40	+ 0	_____
			+ _____

3. 439 + 520

_____

4. 731 + 176

_____

5. 156 + 432

_____

Name _____

Practice
3-1

Adding with an Expanded Algorithm

In **1–4** find each sum.

1. 134 + 221

Hundreds	Tens	Ones
100	30	4
+ 200	+ 20	+ 1
_____	_____	_____

Total

_____
_____
+_____

2. 226 + 423

Hundreds	Tens	Ones
200	20	6
+ 400	+ 20	+ 3
_____	_____	_____

Total

_____
_____
+_____

3. 344 + 421

_____

4. 575 + 342

_____

5. **Persevere** Mac wants to find 291 + 407. He adds the hundreds, tens, and ones. Then, he adds those sums together. What sums did Mac add to find the answer?

_____

6. At Green School, 325 students walk, bike, or get a ride to school. There are 413 students who take the bus to school. How many students go to Green School?

_____

7. **Generalize** Lauren is trying to find how far her family traveled on a road trip. On the first day, they drove 436 miles. On the second day, they drove 342 miles. How many miles did Lauren's family drive in all? Explain how you found the answer.

_____
_____
_____
_____

8. Which of the following shows the sums of the hundreds, tens, and ones for 627 + 361?

A 800 + 80 + 9 **B** 800 + 90 + 8 **C** 900 + 80 + 8 **D** 900 + 90 + 8

P 3·1

Copyright © Pearson Education, Inc., or its affiliates. All Rights Reserved. 3

Models for Adding
3-Digit Numbers

Find 152 + 329.

Step 1: Show each number with place-value blocks.

152

+329

2 ones + 9 ones = 11 ones = 11
5 tens + 2 tens = 7 tens = 70
1 hundred + 3 hundreds = 4 hundreds = 400

Step 2: Combine the ones.   2 + 9 = 11

Step 3: Combine the tens.   50 + 20 = 70

Step 4: Combine the hundreds.   100 + 300 = 400

Step 5: Add.   400 + 70 + 11 = 481

Write each problem and find the sum.

1. _____

2. _____

3. _____

4. _____

Name _____

Models for Adding 3-Digit Numbers

Write each problem and find the sum.

1. _____

2. _____

3. **Number Sense** Ed wants to show 137 + 429 with place-value blocks. He has enough hundreds and ones blocks but only 4 tens blocks. Can he show the problem? Explain.

_____

_____

4. Museum A has 127 steps. Museum B has 194 steps. How many steps do the museums have all together? Place-value blocks may help. _____

5. The country of Malta has an area of 316 square miles. The country of Saint Kitts and Nevis has an area of 261 square miles. What is the area of the two countries all together?

_____ square miles

6. The longest vertical lift drawbridge in the United States is the Arthur Kill Bridge at 558 feet. The longest steel truss bridge in the United States is the Glade Creek Bridge. The Glade Creek Bridge is 226 feet longer than the Arthur Kill Bridge. How many feet long is the Glade Creek Bridge? _____ feet

7. Larry was playing a board game. Larry scored 273 points on the first game and 248 points on the second game. How many points did Larry score in all?

   A 411   **B** 421   **C** 511   **D** 521

Practice **3-2**

P 3·2

3

Name _____

Adding 3-Digit Numbers

Find 237 + 186.

Step 1: Add the ones. 7 ones + 6 ones = 13 ones

Regroup. 13 ones = 1 ten, 3 ones

Step 2: Add the tens. 1 ten + 3 tens + 8 tens = 12 tens

Regroup. 12 tens = 1 hundred, 2 tens

Step 3: Add the hundreds.

1 hundred + 2 hundreds + 1 hundred = 4 hundreds

Add together the hundreds, tens, and ones.

   400 + 20 + 3 = 423

Estimate by rounding to the nearest hundred. Then find each sum.

1.	118	**2.**	283	**3.**	542	**4.**	220
	+ 146		+ 147		+ 109		+ 479

5. Find the sum of 456 and 238.   _____

6. Add 109 and 656.   _____

7. Estimation Estimate to decide which sum is
   less than 600: 356 + 292 or 214 + 356.   _____

Adding 3-Digit Numbers

Estimate. Then find each sum.

1. 329 + 468	**2.** 148 + 231	**3.** 555 + 222	**4.** 472 + 515	**5.** 396 + 428

6. 645 + 79	**7.** 536 + 399	**8.** 268 + 422	**9.** 633 + 210

10. Critical Thinking Follow the steps below to find how many combined points were scored by Howie and Theo.

Points Scored

Player	Points
Howie	272
Theo	325
Isabel	288

   a. Write a number sentence to show how to solve the problem.

   _____

   b. Estimate the total points scored by Howie and Theo.

   _____

   c. Find the actual total. _____

11. Explain It Write an addition story for two 3-digit numbers. Write the answer to your story.

_____

12. Sharon can run 278 yards in one minute. Pete can run 145 more yards than Sharon in one minute. How many yards can Pete run in one minute?

_____

13. There were 752 people at a town meeting last week. There were 163 more people this week. How many people attended this week's meeting?

   A 815   **B** 825   **C** 915   **D** 925

Adding 3 or More Numbers

Find 137 + 201 + 109.

To add three numbers, you can add two numbers first.
Then add the sum of the first two numbers and the
third number.

Step 1	**Step 2**
Add 137 + 201.	Add 338 + 109.

137	1
$\underline{+\ 201}$	338
338	$\underline{+\ 109}$
	447

So, 137 + 201 + 109 = 447.

Find each sum.

1.	32	**2.**	127	**3.**	293	**4.**	358
	64		39		312		427
	$\underline{+\ 71}$		$\underline{+\ \ 87}$		$\underline{+\ \ 78}$		$\underline{+\ 127}$

5. 382 + 45 + 181 = _____

6. 52 + 238 + 76 = _____

7. Number Sense Ranier has 37 baseball cards, 65 football
cards, and 151 hockey cards. How many sports cards
does he have in all? Explain how you found your answer.

_____

_____

Name _____

Adding 3 or More Numbers

1.
```
  75
  36
+ 58
```

2.
```
  142
  297
+ 116
```

3.
```
  524
   97
+ 176
```

4.
```
  273
  187
   64
+ 249
```

5.
```
  319
   48
  136
+ 347
```

6. 237 + 75 + 49

7. 49 + 7 + 63 + 8

8. 143 + 47 + 219 + 136

_____   _____   _____

9. **Estimation** Estimate the sum of 327 + 419 + 173.

_____

10. **Number Sense** Justine has 162 red buttons, 98 blue buttons, and 284 green buttons. She says she knows she has more than 500 buttons without adding. Do you agree? Explain.

_____

_____

11. Carlos ate or drank everything that is listed in the table. How many calories did Carlos consume?

Food	Amount	Calories
Bran flakes	1 ounce	90
Banana	1	105
Orange juice	1 cup	110
Milk	1 cup	150

_____

12. In winning the 1884 U.S. presidential election, Grover Cleveland received 219 electoral votes. He received 168 electoral votes in 1888, and lost. Then he received 277 electoral votes and won in 1892. How many electoral votes did Cleveland receive in all?

_____

13. Kyle has 378 pennies, 192 nickels, and 117 dimes. How many coins does he have all together?

A 495   B 570   C 677   D 687

P 3·4

Name _____

Problem Solving: Draw a Picture

Don sold 18 watermelons in the morning and 14 in the afternoon. How many watermelons did he sell in all?

You can draw a rectangle to show addition.

Each part of the rectangle represents one of the addends. Add the parts to show how many in all.

Don sold 32 watermelons in all.

---

1. Two buses are carrying students to a field trip. There are 36 students on one bus and 30 students on the other. How many students are on the buses in all?

```
|——————— students in all ———————|
| 36              | 30             |
      ↑                  ↑
   Bus #1             Bus #2
```

2. **Estimation** Vanessa bought a sweater for $27 and a skirt for $22. About how much money did Vanessa spend in all?

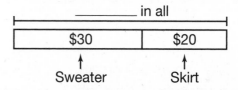

3. A pet store sold 26 puppies and 14 kittens last month. How many animals were sold in all?

```
|——————— animals in all ———————|
| 26              | 14             |
```

4. Ken has 15 rap CDs, 20 country CDs, and 30 rock CDs. How many CDs does Ken have in all?

```
|——————— CDs in all ———————|
| 15   | 20    | 30         |
```

Name _____

Problem Solving: Draw a Picture

1. Kelly bought a CD for $15 and a book for $13. How much money did Kelly spend in all?

   ```
   |_____ in all_____|
   |   $15    |    $13      |
        ↑            ↑
   Cost of CD   Cost of book
   ```

2. **Estimation** There are 28 students in the chorus and 31 students in the band. All will be performing tonight. About how many students will be performing in all?

   ```
   |_____ students in all_____|
   |    30     |     30     |
        ↑            ↑
     Chorus        Band
   ```

3. Jane sold 25 raffle tickets Monday, 30 raffle tickets Tuesday, and 40 raffle tickets Wednesday. How many raffle tickets did Jane sell all together?

   ```
   |_____ tickets in all_____|
   |  25  |  30  |  40  |
   ```

4. Dan cycled 12 miles Saturday and 18 miles Sunday. How many miles did he cycle all together?

   ```
   |_____ miles in all_____|
   |    12    |    18    |
   ```

The table shows the number of students who belong to clubs. Use the table for **5** through **7**.

5. How many students belong to the Spanish and Science clubs?

   ```
   |_____ members in all_____|
   |          |          |
   ```

| Club Membership ||
Club	Members
Math	24
Spanish	18
Running	15
Science	6

6. About how many students belong to the Math and Spanish clubs?

   ```
   |_____ members in all_____|
   |          |          |
   ```

7. How many students belong to the Math, Running, and Science clubs?

   ```
   |_____ members in all_____|
   |        |        |        |
   ```

Subtracting with an Expanded Algorithm

Apple Hill is 568 feet high. Banana Hill is 293 feet high. How many feet higher is Apple Hill than Banana Hill?

Find 568 − 293.

"I need to find 568 − 293."

Step 1	**Step 2**	**Step 3**
568 − 293 = ?	Now, start with 368.	Start with 278.
Start with 568.	Subtract the **9 tens** in 293.	Subtract the **3 ones** in 293.
Subtract the **2 hundreds** in 293.	There are not enough tens. So, subtract the **6 tens** that are there.	278 − 3 = 275
568 − 200 = 368	368 − 60 = 308	In all 200 + 60 + 30 + 3 = 293 has been subtracted.
So far, 200 has been subtracted.	Then, subtract the tens that are left.	Apple Hill is 275 feet higher than Banana Hill.
	9 tens − 6 tens = 3 tens	
	308 − 30 = 278	
	So far, 200 + 60 + 30 = 290 has been subtracted.	

1. Follow these steps to find 576 − 471.
First subtract 400.
Then, subtract 70.
Then, subtract 1.

2. Follow these steps to find 365 − 138.
First subtract 100.
Then, subtract 30.
Then, subtract 5.
Then, subtract 3.

_____

_____

3. Find 756 − 602.

4. Find 848 − 276.

5. Find 641 − 139.

_____

_____

_____

6. Sue's story is 367 words long. Rob's story is 296 words long. How many more words does Sue's story have than Rob's?

7. **Reason** Find 496 − 217. Were there enough ones to subtract? How did you know?

_____

_____

Subtracting with an Expanded Algorithm

1. Follow these steps to find
   $879 - 659$.
   First subtract 600.
   Then, subtract 50.
   Then, subtract 9.

   _____

2. Follow these steps to find
   $775 - 431$.
   First subtract 400.
   Then, subtract 30.
   Then, subtract 1.

   _____

3. Follow these steps to find
   $564 - 117$.
   First subtract 100.
   Then, subtract 10.
   Then, subtract 4.
   Then, subtract 3.

   _____

4. Follow these steps to find
   $428 - 275$.
   First subtract 200.
   Then, subtract 20.
   Then, subtract 50.
   Then, subtract 5.

   _____

5. Find $684 - 362$.

   _____

6. Find $208 - 135$.

   _____

7. Find $479 - 283$.

   _____

8. Find $614 - 153$.

   _____

9. Eric and Kim are on a game show.
   Eric has 583 points. Kim has
   349 points. How many more
   points does Eric have than Kim?

   _____

10. **Reason** Malcolm is trying to find
    $775 - 342$. He subtracts hundreds
    first, then tens, then ones. What
    three numbers did Malcolm
    subtract to find the answer?

    _____

11. **Communicate** Kyle is making a building out of blocks. So far his
    building is made up of 129 blocks. When his building is finished,
    it will have 275 blocks. How many more blocks does Kyle need to
    finish his building? Explain how you found your answer.

    _____

    _____

12. Which of the following shows the numbers that can be subtracted to find
    $395 - 129$?

    A 300, 90, 5   **B** 900, 20, 1   **C** 100, 20, 9, 5   **D** 100, 20, 5, 4

Models for Subtracting 3-Digit Numbers

You can use place-value blocks to subtract.

Find 234 − 192.

Estimate: 230 − 190 = 40, so the answer should be about 40.

What You Show	What You Write
Step 1 Show 234 with place-value blocks.	234 −192
Step 2 Subtract the ones. 4 > 2. No regrouping is needed. 4 ones − 2 ones = 2 ones	234 −192 2
Step 3 Subtract the tens. 3 tens < 9 tens, so regroup 1 hundred for 10 tens. 13 tens − 9 tens = 4 tens	1 13 2̶34 −192 42
Step 4 Subtract the hundreds. 1 hundred − 1 hundred = 0 hundreds	1 13 2̶34 −192 42

Find the value of the remaining blocks:

4 tens + 2 ones = 40 + 2 = 42

So, 234 − 192 = 42.

Use place-value blocks or draw pictures to subtract.

1.	156 − 28	**2.**	261 − 122	**3.**	321 − 76	**4.**	446 − 257

Models for Subtracting 3-Digit Numbers

Use the place-value blocks to subtract.

1.
232
− 147

2.
324
− 156

Use place-value blocks or draw pictures to subtract.

3. 321
     − 176

4. 242
     − 86

5. 332
     − 117

6. 267
     − 149

7. 413
     − 237

8. 165
     − 137

9. 251
     − 137

10. 372
      − 283

11. 511
      − 324

12. 346
      − 138

For **13** and **14**, use the table at the right.

13. What is the difference between the greatest and least number of pages read? _____

14. How many more pages did Lance read than Annie? _____

Pages Read	
Name	**Pages Read**
Lance	322
Annie	263
Brad	415

15. Number Sense Edie wanted to subtract 273 − 188. She began by finding 2−1. What did Edie do wrong?

_____

_____

16. Alice defeated Ralph 313 to 188 in a board game. By how many points did Alice win?

A 115   **B** 125   **C** 215   **D** 225

Subtracting 3-Digit Numbers

Find 726 − 238.

Estimate: 700 − 200 = 500, so the answer should be about 500.

Step 1	**Step 2**	**Step 3**
First subtract the ones. Regroup 1 ten into 10 ones.	Subtract the tens. Regroup 1 hundred into 10 tens.	Subtract the hundreds.

Step 1

$$\begin{array}{r} 1\ 16 \\ 72\cancel{6} \\ -238 \\ \hline 8 \end{array}$$

Step 2

$$\begin{array}{r} 11 \\ 6\ \cancel{1}\ 16 \\ 7\cancel{2}\cancel{6} \\ -238 \\ \hline 88 \end{array}$$

Step 3

$$\begin{array}{r} 11 \\ 6\ \cancel{1}\ 16 \\ 7\cancel{2}\cancel{6} \\ -238 \\ \hline 488 \end{array}$$

Is your answer correct?
Check by adding:
488 + 238 = 726.
It checks.

Find each difference. Estimate and check answers for reasonableness.

1. 318
    − 123

2. 441
    − 187

3. 334
    − 275

4. 512
    − 299

5. 423 − 156 = _____

6. 327 − 159 = _____

7. The town library had 634 CDs for rent. During one week, 288 of them were rented. How many CDs were left?

    _____

8. **Number Sense** If you had to subtract 426 from 913, how many times would you need to regroup? How can you tell?

    _____

    _____

    _____

    _____

Name _____

Subtracting 3-Digit Numbers

Find each difference. Estimate and check answers for reasonableness.

1. 732 − 328	**2.** 621 − 153	**3.** 369 − 185	**4.** 267 − 78	**5.** 527 − 279

6. 917 − 436	**7.** 555 − 189	**8.** 422 − 244	**9.** 853 − 456	**10.** 451 − 363

11. 527 − 242 = _____ **12.** 746 − 437 = _____ **13.** 941 − 267 = _____

14. Tulsa is how many miles closer to Omaha than Dallas? _____

15. Tulsa is how many miles closer to Omaha than Chicago? _____

All Roads Lead to Omaha

Start	Finish	Miles
Dallas	Omaha	644
Chicago	Omaha	459
Tulsa	Omaha	387

16. Strategy Practice Jill is going on a trip from Chicago to Omaha to Tulsa. Bill will travel from Dallas to Omaha. How much farther will Jill travel than Bill?

a. What do you need to do first?

_____

_____

b. What is the next step?

_____

c. Solve the problem.
_____ miles

17. Texas has 254 counties. California has 58 counties and Florida has 67 counties. How many more counties does Texas have than California and Florida combined?

A 125   **B** 129   **C** 139   **D** 196

Subtracting Across Zero

To subtract from a number with 0 in the tens place, you need to regroup one hundred into 10 tens.

Find $207 - 98$.

Step 1	Step 2	Step 3
Subtract the ones. Since there are 0 tens, you must first regroup the hundreds.	Regroup the hundreds. 2 hundreds and 0 tens = 1 hundred and 10 tens.	Regroup the tens. 10 tens and 7 ones = 9 tens and 17 ones. Subtract.
$\begin{array}{r} 207 \\ -\ 98 \\ \hline \end{array}$	$\begin{array}{r} {\scriptstyle 1\,10} \\ 2\not0 7 \\ -\ 98 \\ \hline \end{array}$	$\begin{array}{r} {\scriptstyle 9} \\ {\scriptstyle 1\,10\,17} \\ 2\not0\not7 \\ -\ 98 \\ \hline 109 \end{array}$

Is your answer correct? Check by adding: $109 + 98 = 207$.

Find each difference.

1. $\begin{array}{r} 301 \\ -\ 72 \\ \hline \end{array}$
2. $\begin{array}{r} 205 \\ -\ 36 \\ \hline \end{array}$
3. $\begin{array}{r} 400 \\ -\ 228 \\ \hline \end{array}$
4. $\begin{array}{r} 502 \\ -\ 225 \\ \hline \end{array}$
5. $\begin{array}{r} 603 \\ -\ 215 \\ \hline \end{array}$

6. $307 - 149 =$ _____
7. $702 - 259 =$ _____
8. $504 - 397 =$ _____

9. **Number Sense** Waco has an elevation of 405 feet above sea level. Texarkana has an elevation of 324 feet above sea level. How many feet greater is Waco's elevation than Texarkana's? Show your work.

_____ feet

Subtracting Across Zero

Find each difference.

1. 406 − 28	**2.** 300 − 211	**3.** 501 − 268	**4.** 705 − 347	**5.** 605 − 219

6. 800 − 579	**7.** 907 − 728	**8.** 603 − 347	**9.** 507 − 388	**10.** 706 − 497

11. 404 − 305 = _____ **12.** 501 − 223 = _____ **13.** 302 − 166 = _____

14. There were 600 ears of corn for sale at the produce market. At the end of the day, there were 212 ears left. How many ears of corn were sold? _____

15. Darrin has 702 CDs in his collection. Dana has 357 CDs in her collection. How many more CDs does Darrin have than Dana? _____

16. Strategy Practice Party Palace has an order for 505 party favors. It packaged 218 favors on Saturday and 180 favors on Sunday. How many more party favors does it still need to package? _____

17. Write a Problem Write a subtraction problem involving regrouping that has Ted reading 304 pages. Answer your question.

_____

_____

_____

18. The Williams Tower in Houston, TX, is 901 feet tall. The Tower of the Americas in San Antonio, TX, is 622 feet tall. How much taller is the Williams Tower than the Tower of the Americas?

A 279 feet   **B** 289 feet   **C** 379 feet   **D** 389 feet

Making Sense of Addition Equations

An **equation** is a number sentence that uses an equal sign (=) to show that the value to its left is the same as the value to its right.

12 + 4 = 16 is an example of an equation.

Some equations have letters in them or *unknowns*.

$$9 = n + 2$$

This equation means: 9 is equal to some number + 2

You can find the value of *n* that makes the equation true or equal on each side by thinking of addition or subtraction facts.

Think: You know that 7 + 2 = 9, so *n* = 7.

In **1–8,** write a basic fact that is related to each equation. Then find the value for *n* that makes the equation true.

1. 18 = 9 + *n*   **2.** *n* + 6 = 10   **3.** 12 = 7 + *n*   **4.** 6 + *n* = 6

_____   _____   _____   _____

_____   _____   _____   _____

5. 14 = 6 + *n*   **6.** *n* + 5 = 6   **7.** 13 = 7 + *n*   **8.** 10 + *n* = 17

_____   _____   _____   _____

_____   _____   _____   _____

9. Critique Reasoning Fred decides that 12 + 40 = 62 is NOT a true equation. Is Fred correct? Explain.

_____

Making Sense of Addition Equations

In **1–8**, decide if the two sides are equal. If *yes*, write =.
If *no*, write ≠ (not equal).

1. $9 \bigcirc 5 + 4$

2. $10 + 3 \bigcirc 5$

3. $23 + 6 \bigcirc 29$

4. $12 \bigcirc 13 + 5$

_____

_____

_____

_____

5. $9 + 2 \bigcirc 7$

6. $14 \bigcirc 5 + 9$

7. $33 \bigcirc 14 + 19$

8. $14 + 4 \bigcirc 18$

_____

_____

_____

_____

In **9–16**, find the value for *n* that makes the equation true.

9. $16 = 7 + n$

10. $12 = n + 2$

11. $8 = 5 + n$

12. $n + 5 = 14$

_____

_____

_____

_____

13. $7 + n = 7$

14. $14 + n = 14$

15. $n = 45 + 6$

16. $8 = 6 + n$

_____

_____

_____

_____

For **17** and **18**, use the given equation to solve the problem.

17. Dina has 5 orchids. Mae has 13 orchids. How many more orchids does Mae have than Dina?

$5 + n = 13$

_____

18. Fran collected 7 more stamps than Erin. Fran collected 24 stamps. How many stamps did Erin collect?

$n + 7 = 24$

_____

19. **Model** Derrick has 7 marbles. Roger has *n* marbles. Together they have 14 marbles. Write an equation to model the problem. How many marbles does Roger have?

_____

20. Which value for *n* makes the equation $n + 8 = 45$ true?

A $n = 37$ **C** $n = 41$

B $n = 38$ **D** $n = 53$

Name _____

Making Sense of Subtraction Equations

An **equation** is a number sentence that uses an equal sign (=) to show that the value to its left is the same as the value to its right.

$18 - 6 = 12$ is an example of an equation.

Some equations have letters in them or *unknowns*.

$$9 = n - 4$$

This equation means: 9 is equal to some number $- 4$

You can find the value of n that makes the equation true or equal on each side by thinking of addition or subtraction facts.

Think: You know that $13 - 4 = 9$, so $n = 13$.

In **1–8,** write a basic fact that is related to each equation. Then find the value for n that makes the equation true.

1. $18 = 22 - n$ **2.** $n - 4 = 2$ **3.** $12 = 12 - n$ **4.** $3 - n = 3$

_____   _____   _____   _____

_____   _____   _____   _____

5. $6 = 15 - n$ **6.** $n - 5 = 6$ **7.** $6 = 7 - n$ **8.** $10 - n = 7$

_____   _____   _____   _____

_____   _____   _____   _____

9. Critique Reasoning Ken decides that $21 - 6 = 14$ is NOT a true equation. Is Ken correct? Explain.

_____

Making Sense of Subtraction Equations

In **1–8**, decide if the two sides are equal. If *yes*, write =.
If *no*, write ≠ (not equal).

1. $9 \bigcirc 16 - 7$ **2.** $10 - 4 \bigcirc 5$ **3.** $41 - 12 \bigcirc 29$ **4.** $12 \bigcirc 14 - 1$

_____   _____   _____   _____

5. $18 - 12 \bigcirc 7$ **6.** $14 \bigcirc 17 - 3$ **7.** $33 \bigcirc 44 - 11$ **8.** $27 - 9 \bigcirc 18$

_____   _____   _____   _____

In **9–16**, find the value for *n* that makes the equation true.

9. $7 = 16 - n$ **10.** $12 = n - 3$ **11.** $20 = 32 - n$ **12.** $n - 6 = 3$

_____   _____   _____   _____

13. $8 - n = 8$ **14.** $24 - n = 14$ **15.** $n = 45 - 6$ **16.** $8 = 10 - n$

_____   _____   _____   _____

For **17** and **18**, use the given equation to solve the problem.

17. Mia has 8 roses. Linda has 13 roses. How many fewer roses does Mia have than Linda?

$13 - n = 8$

_____

18. Juan collected 7 fewer rocks than Jenn. Juan collected 24 rocks. How many rocks did Jenn collect?

$n - 7 = 24$

_____

19. Model Bill has 18 coins. He uses some coins. Now he has 7 left. How many coins did he use? Write an equation to model the problem.

_____

20. Which value for *n* makes the equation $n - 12 = 26$ true?

A $n = 37$ **C** $n = 43$

B $n = 38$ **D** $n = 56$

Adding and Subtracting

Addition and subtraction are related.

$$12 - 5 = 7$$
$$7 + 5 = 12$$

You can use addition to check subtraction.
You can use subtraction to check addition.

Subtract $900 - 534$. Estimate: $900 - 500 = 400$

Step 1

Regroup hundreds to tens and tens to ones.

Step 2

Check your work.
Since you subtracted,
use addition to check.

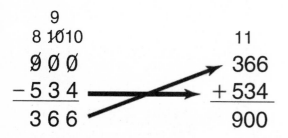

```
    9
  8 10 10
  9  0  0
- 5  3  4
  3  6  6
```

```
     11
    366
  + 534
    900
```

Use the difference as one addend. Use the number you subtracted as the other addend. The sum should match the number you subtracted from.

366 is the correct difference.

In **1** and **2**, add or subtract. Use the inverse operation to check your answer.

1. $\begin{array}{r} 400 \\ -165 \end{array}$ ⟶ $\begin{array}{r} 235 \\ +165 \end{array}$

2. $\begin{array}{r} 514 \\ +317 \end{array}$ ⟶ $\begin{array}{r} 831 \\ -317 \end{array}$

In **3** and **4**, find the sum or difference. Fill in the numbers in the problem you used to check your answer.

3. $\begin{array}{r} 906 \\ -641 \end{array}$ ⟶ $\begin{array}{r} \underline{} \\ + \underline{} \end{array}$

4. $\begin{array}{r} 251 \\ +749 \end{array}$ ⟶ $\begin{array}{r} \underline{} \\ - \underline{} \end{array}$

5. **Draw a Picture** Cara's goal is to have 800 buttons in her collection. She already has 327 buttons. How many more buttons does she need to reach her goal? Draw a picture to help solve the problem.

Name _____

Adding and Subtracting

In **1–3,** find the sum or difference. Write the operation you can use to check your answer.

1. $606 - 259$ **2.** $432 + 568$ **3.** $832 - 427$

In **4–7,** estimate, then find the sum or difference. Use the inverse operation to check your answer.

4. $\begin{array}{r} 890 \\ -\ 623 \\ \hline \end{array}$ **5.** $\begin{array}{r} 786 \\ -\ 465 \\ \hline \end{array}$ **6.** $\begin{array}{r} 318 \\ +\ 473 \\ \hline \end{array}$ **7.** $\begin{array}{r} 192 \\ +\ 808 \\ \hline \end{array}$

Use the table for **8** and **9**.

8. How many more orange cartons than grapefruit cartons did the Sun Citrus Company ship?

_____

**Sun Citrus Company
Citrus Fruits Shipped**

Fruit	Number of Cartons
Grapefruits	370
Oranges	501
Tangelos	264

9. What is the total number of orange cartons and tangelo cartons the company shipped?

_____

10. Jon's goal is to have 500 shells in his collection. He already has 295 shells. How many more shells does he need to collect?

  A 205   **B** 305   **C** 315   **D** 795

11. Writing to Explain Elsa added $579 + 234$ and got 813. Then she used $813 + 234$ to check her answer. Explain what she did wrong.

_____

_____

Problem Solving: Draw a Picture and Write a Number Sentence

The distance from Cleveland, OH, to Pittsburgh, PA, is 129 miles. Detroit, MI, is 170 miles away from Cleveland. How much closer is Cleveland to Pittsburgh than to Detroit?

You can subtract to find how many miles closer Cleveland is to Pittsburgh than to Detroit.

170 miles	
129	?

$$\begin{array}{r} 170 \\ -\ 129 \\ \hline 41 \end{array}$$

Cleveland is 41 miles closer to Pittsburgh than to Detroit.

You can estimate $170 - 130 = 40$ to show that the answer is reasonable.

Solve.

1. Honolulu, HI, has an area of 86 square miles. Corpus Christi, TX, has an area that is 69 square miles greater than the area of Honolulu. How many square miles is Corpus Christi?

   _____ square miles

86	69

2. Bakersfield, CA, has an area of 113 square miles. Its area is 64 square miles greater than the area of Anaheim, CA. What is the area, in square miles, of Anaheim?

   113 square miles

3. **Writing to Explain** How did you know which operation to use to solve Problem 2?

   _____

   _____

   _____

Problem Solving: Draw a Picture and Write a Number Sentence

The table below shows the areas of some of the smallest countries in the world. Use the table for **1–3.**

1. How many square miles greater is Maldives than San Marino?

116 square miles

| 24 | _____ |

Area of Countries

Country	Area (in sq mi)
San Marino	24
Liechtenstein	62
Maldives	116
Palau	177

2. **Draw a Picture** Draw a diagram to show how to find the difference between the areas of Liechtenstein and San Marino. Use your diagram to solve the problem.

3. Grenada is 15 square miles greater than Maldives. What is the area of Grenada?

_____ square miles

| 116 | 15 |

4. There are 237 students at Johnson Elementary School. There are 188 students at Hoover Elementary School. How many more students are at Johnson than at Hoover?

237 students

| 188 | _____ |

5. **Write a Problem** Write a real-world problem that you can solve by adding or subtracting. Then give your problem to a classmate to solve.

_____

_____

_____

Multiplication as Repeated Addition

Each group below has the same number of squares. There are 5 groups of 4 squares. There are a total of 20 squares.

Here is the addition sentence for this problem: $4 + 4 + 4 + 4 + 4 = 20$

Here is the multiplication sentence for this problem: $5 \times 4 = 20$

Complete the addition and multiplication sentences.

1. ○○ ○○ ○○ ○○
○○ ○○ ○○ ○○

4 groups of _____ $4 + 4 + 4 + 4 =$ _____ $4 \times$ _____ $= 16$

2. ○○○○ ○○○○ ○○○○ ○○○○
○○○ ○○○ ○○○ ○○○

_____ groups of 7   _____ + _____ + _____ + _____ = 28

_____ $\times 7 =$ _____

Write each addition sentence as a multiplication sentence.

3. $1 + 1 + 1 + 1 + 1 = 5$ _____

4. $8 + 8 + 8 = 24$ _____

Write each multiplication sentence as an addition sentence.

5. $5 \times 5 = 25$ _____

6. $6 \times 2 = 12$ _____

7. Communicate Juan says, "When you put together unequal groups, you can only add." Is he correct? Explain.

_____

Multiplication as Repeated Addition

Complete.

1. ⬤⬤⬤⬤⬤
⬤⬤⬤⬤⬤

2. ⬤⬤⬤⬤
⬤⬤⬤⬤
⬤⬤⬤⬤

2 groups of _____

3 groups of _____

$5 +$ _____ $=$ _____

$4 +$ _____ $+$ _____ $=$ _____

$2 \times$ _____ $=$ _____

$3 \times$ _____ $=$ _____

3. $4 + 4 + 4 + 4 + 4 = 5 \times$ _____

4. _____ $+$ _____ $+$ _____ $= 3 \times 8$

5. $9 +$ _____ $+$ _____ $=$ _____ $\times 9$

6. $7 + 7 + 7 + 7 =$ _____ $\times$ _____

Write $+$, $-$, or $\times$ for each ☐.

7. $5 \;\boxed{}\; 4 = 9$

8. $6 \;\boxed{}\; 2 = 12$

9. $7 \;\boxed{}\; 3 = 4$

10. $3 \;\boxed{}\; 3 = 9$

11. $8 \;\boxed{}\; 6 = 2$

12. $3 \;\boxed{}\; 3 = 6$

13. Reason Marlon has 4 cards, Jake has 4 cards, and Sam has 3 cards. Can you write a multiplication sentence to find how many cards they have in all? Explain.

_____

_____

14. Write a Problem Draw a picture that shows equal groups. Then write an addition sentence and a multiplication sentence for your picture.

15. Which is equal to $6 + 6 + 6 + 6$?

A 6×3 **B** 3×6 **C** 4×6 **D** 6×5

P 4·1

Arrays and Multiplication

Multiplication can be used to find the total in an array.

Scott arranged some apples in an array. He made 4 rows with 3 apples in each row. How many apples does Scott have?

Draw Scott's array.

The array shows 4 rows of 3 apples.

$3 + 3 + 3 + 3 = 12$

Say, 4 times 3 equals 12

Write, $4 \times 3 = 12$

Scott has 12 apples.

Write a multiplication sentence for each array.

1.

_____

2.

_____

3.

_____

4. Draw an array to show the fact 3×4.

5. Model Priya is arranging 28 chairs with 7 chairs in each row. How many rows will there be? You can use an array to help.

_____

Arrays and Multiplication

Write a multiplication sentence for each array.

1.   **2.**   **3.**

_____ × _____ = _____   _____ × _____ = _____   _____ × _____ = _____

Draw an array to show each multiplication fact. Write the product.

4. $2 \times 8 =$ _____   **5.** $3 \times 6 =$ _____

6. Model Paula arranged her stamps in an album. The album has
3 rows with 7 stamps in each row. How many stamps
does Paula have? Draw an array to solve your problem.

_____

7. Jonathan is arranging 36 pictures, with 9 pictures in each row.
How many rows will there be?

A 9   **B** 5   **C** 4   **D** 2

The Commutative Property

An array shows objects in equal rows.
This array shows 3 rows of 6 pennies.

The multiplication sentence for this array is
$3 \times 6 = 18$.

You can use the Commutative (Order)
Property of Multiplication to multiply the
numbers in any order:
$3 \times 6 = 18$ and $6 \times 3 = 18$.

Write a multiplication sentence for each array.

1. ○○○○○○○
○○○○○○○

2. ☐☐☐☐
☐☐☐☐
☐☐☐☐
☐☐☐☐

_____   _____

Complete each multiplication sentence. You may use counters or
draw a picture to help.

3. $3 \times 4 = 12$ _____ $\times 3 = 12$ **4.** $5 \times 2 = 10$ $2 \times$ _____ $= 10$

5. Number Sense How can you use the Commutative Property to know that

○○○○○○
○○○○○○   is equal to
○○○○○○

○○○
○○○
○○○
○○○
○○○
○○○   ?

_____

_____

_____

The Commutative Property

Write a multiplication sentence for each array.

1. OOOOO
OOOOO
OOOOO

2. OOOOOOOOO
OOOOOOOOO

3. OOOOOO
OOOOOO
OOOOOO
OOOOOO

_____   _____   _____

Draw an array to find each multiplication fact. Write the product.

4. $3 \times 6 =$ _____

5. $4 \times 7 =$ _____

Complete each multiplication sentence.
Use counters or draw an array to help.

6. $3 \times$ ____ $= 21$

$7 \times$ ____ $= 21$

7. $4 \times 9 =$ ____

$9 \times 4 =$ ____

8. $5 \times 6 =$ ____

$6 \times 5 =$ ____

9. $4 \times 7 =$ ____

$7 \times 4 =$ ____

10. $6 \times 8 =$ ____

$8 \times 6 =$ ____

11. $9 \times 5 =$ ____

$5 \times 9 =$ ____

12. Explain It If you know that $7 \times 8 = 56$, how can you use the Commutative (Order) Property of Multiplication to find the product of 8×7?

_____

_____

_____

_____

13. Which of the following is equal to 8×4?

A 4×8 **B** $4 + 8$ **C** $8 - 4$ **D** $8 + 4$

Problem Solving: Writing to Explain

David is making 3 pancakes for each person in his family. Today, there are 6 family members at breakfast. How many pancakes does he need to make? Explain how you can solve this problem.

You can make a table to solve this problem.

As the number of people increases by 1, the number of pancakes David needs to make increases by 3.

People	1	2	3	4	5	6
Pancakes	3	6	9	12	15	18

| | 3 + 3 = 6 | 6 + 3 = 9 | 9 + 3 = 12 | 12 + 3 = 15 | 15 + 3 = 18 |

David needs to make 18 pancakes.

---

1. Marcia got on an elevator on the fourth floor. She went down 2 floors. Then she went up 6 floors. Then she went down 3 floors. What floor is Marcia on now?

_____

2. Explain It How did you find your answer to Exercise 1?

_____

_____

_____

3. Look at the numbers below.
75, 74, 72, 69, 65, ...

a. Describe the pattern.

_____

_____

_____

b. What are the next two numbers in the pattern?

_____

4. Ms. Skidmore is setting up basketball teams. There are 5 players on each team.

a. Complete the table below.

Teams	1	2	3	4	5
Players	5	10	15		

b. Describe the pattern by how the number of teams and players change.

_____

_____

Problem Solving: Writing to Explain

1. Look at the numbers below.
   13, 15, 19, 25, …

   a. Describe the pattern.

   _____

   _____

   _____

   b. Explain how you can find the next two numbers. What are the next two numbers?

   _____

   _____

2. Mr. Wilson is setting up volleyball teams. There are 6 players on a team.

   a. Complete the table below.

Teams	1	2	3	4	5
Players	6	12	18		

   b. Explain how the number of players changes as the number of teams changes.

   _____

   _____

   _____

3. **Look for Patterns** The table below shows the amount of money that Louise earns in allowance each week.

   a. Complete the table.

   Louise's Allowance

Number of Weeks	Allowance
1	$8
2	$16
3	$24
4	
5	

   b. How did the table help you to find the pattern?

   _____

   _____

4. Diana is training to run a race.

   a. Complete the table for Diana's first week of training.

   Diana's Training Schedule

Day	Minutes
Monday	15
Tuesday	20
Wednesday	25
Thursday	
Friday	

   b. If she continues the pattern, for how many minutes will Diana run on Saturday?

   _____

2 and 5 as Factors

When you multiply by 2, you can use a doubles fact.
For example, 2×3 is the same as adding $3 + 3$.

You can use a pattern to multiply by 5.

2s Facts		5s Facts	
$2 \times 0 = 0$	$2 \times 5 = 10$	$5 \times 0 = 0$	$5 \times 5 = 25$
$2 \times 1 = 2$	$2 \times 6 = 12$	$5 \times 1 = 5$	$5 \times 6 = 30$
$2 \times 2 = 4$	$2 \times 7 = 14$	$5 \times 2 = 10$	$5 \times 7 = 35$
$2 \times 3 = 6$	$2 \times 8 = 16$	$5 \times 3 = 15$	$5 \times 8 = 40$
$2 \times 4 = 8$	$2 \times 9 = 18$	$5 \times 4 = 20$	$5 \times 9 = 45$

Each multiple of 2 ends in 0, 2, 4, 6, or 8. All multiples of 2 are even.

Each multiple of 5 ends in 0 or 5.

Find each product.

1. $3 \times 2 =$ _____

2. $4 \times 2 =$ _____

3. $6 \times 2 =$ _____

4. $4 \times 5 =$ _____

5. $3 \times 5 =$ _____

6. $7 \times 5 =$ _____

7. $5 \times 2 =$ _____

8. $6 \times 5 =$ _____

9. $8 \times 2 =$ _____

10.
$$\begin{array}{r} 9 \\ \times 5 \\ \hline \end{array}$$

11.
$$\begin{array}{r} 2 \\ \times 7 \\ \hline \end{array}$$

12.
$$\begin{array}{r} 2 \\ \times 2 \\ \hline \end{array}$$

13.
$$\begin{array}{r} 5 \\ \times 5 \\ \hline \end{array}$$

14.
$$\begin{array}{r} 0 \\ \times 2 \\ \hline \end{array}$$

15. What is 9 times 2? _____

16. What is 5 times 8? _____

17. **Communicate** Is 25 a multiple of 2 or 5? How do you know?

_____

_____

Name _____

2 and 5 as Factors

Find each product.

1. 2×5 **2.** 4×5 **3.** 3×2 **4.** 8×5 **5.** 7×2

_____   _____   _____   _____   _____

6. $\begin{array}{r} 9 \\ \times\, 2 \\ \hline \end{array}$ **7.** $\begin{array}{r} 6 \\ \times\, 5 \\ \hline \end{array}$ **8.** $\begin{array}{r} 5 \\ \times\, 9 \\ \hline \end{array}$ **9.** $\begin{array}{r} 2 \\ \times\, 6 \\ \hline \end{array}$ **10.** $\begin{array}{r} 5 \\ \times\, 5 \\ \hline \end{array}$

11. Multiply 7 and 5. _____   **12.** Find 8 times 2. _____

Compare. Use $<$, $>$, or $=$.

13. $3 \times 5 \bigcirc 4 \times 5$ **14.** $6 \times 3 \bigcirc 6 \times 2$ **15.** $8 \times 2 \bigcirc 2 \times 8$

16. $6 \times 5 \bigcirc 5 \times 6$ **17.** $4 \times 2 \bigcirc 5 \times 2$ **18.** $7 \times 5 \bigcirc 5 \times 6$

19. Tara walks 2 miles each day. How many miles does she walk in a week?

_____

20. There are 5 days in each school week. How many school days are there in 9 weeks?

_____

21. **Writing to Explain** How can adding doubles help you to multiply by 2? Give an example.

_____

_____

_____

_____

22. If the ones digit of a number greater than 1 is 0, what factor or factors must that number have?

  A 2 only   **B** 5 only   **C** 2 and 5   **D** Neither 2 nor 5

9 as a Factor

You can use two patterns to help you remember 9s facts.

9s Facts
9 × 0 = 0
9 × 1 = 9
9 × 2 = 18
9 × 3 = 27
9 × 4 = 36
9 × 5 = 45
9 × 6 = 54
9 × 7 = 63
9 × 8 = 72
9 × 9 = 81

1. The tens digit will be 1 less than the factor being multiplied by 9.

2. The sum of the digits of the product will always be 9, unless the other factor is 0.

Find 9 × 7.

The tens digit must be 1 less than 7.
The tens digit is 6.

The sum of the digits must be 9.
9 − 6 = 3, so the ones digit is 3.

The product is 63.

Find each product.

1. 9 × 3 = _____

2. 2 × 9 = _____

3. 1 × 9 = _____

4. 5 × 9 = _____

5. 5 × 8 = _____

6. 6 × 9 = _____

7. 2 × 7 = _____

8. 0 × 9 = _____

9. 4 × 9 = _____

10. 9
     × 9

11. 9
     × 5

12. 8
     × 9

13. 7
     × 9

14. 9
     × 2

15. Multiply 6 and 9. _____

16. Multiply 0 and 9. _____

17. Communicate Look at the table of 9s facts. Do you see another number pattern in the multiples of 9? Explain.

_____

_____

9 as a Factor

Find each product.

1. 9×4 **2.** 7×9 **3.** 9×9 **4.** 9×8 **5.** 5×3

_____   _____   _____   _____   _____

6. 9 **7.** 2 **8.** 6 **9.** 2 **10.** 8

   $\times 5$ $\times 9$ $\times 9$ $\times 7$ $\times 9$

11. Multiply 4 and 9. _____   **12.** Find 3 times 9. _____

Complete. Use $+$, $-$, or $\times$.

13. $2 \times 9 = 10 \boxed{} 8$ **14.** $20 + 16 = 9 \boxed{} 4$ **15.** $9 \times 5 = 50 \boxed{} 5$

16. $9 \times 8 = 70 \boxed{} 2$ **17.** $10 \boxed{} 1 = 1 \times 9$ **18.** $9 \boxed{} 3 = 20 + 7$

19. Paula's hair was put into 9 braids. Each braid used 3 beads. How many beads were used in all?

_____

20. A baseball game has 9 innings. A doubleheader is 2 games in the same day. How many innings are there in a doubleheader?

_____

21. **Write a Problem** Write a multiplication story for 9×8. Include the product in your story.

_____

_____

22. Which number below is a multiple of 9?

A 35   **B** 46   **C** 54   **D** 65

Multiplying with 0 and 1

Zero and one have special multiplication properties.

The Identity (One) Property of Multiplication	The Zero Property of Multiplication
When you multiply a number and 1, the product is that number. Examples: $4 \times 1 = 4$ $16 \times 1 = 16$ $1 \times 9 = 9$ $13 \times 1 = 13$ $251 \times 1 = 251$ $1 \times 48 = 48$	When you multiply a number and 0, the product is 0. Examples: $5 \times 0 = 0$ $123 \times 0 = 0$ $17 \times 0 = 0$ $0 \times 58 = 0$ $0 \times 51 = 0$ $74 \times 0 = 0$

1. $1 \times 2 =$ _____

2. $0 \times 3 =$ _____

3. $4 \times 1 =$ _____

4. $8 \times 0 =$ _____

5. $6 \times 1 =$ _____

6. $1 \times 7 =$ _____

7. $\begin{array}{r} 1 \\ \times\ 7 \\ \hline \end{array}$

8. $\begin{array}{r} 6 \\ \times\ 0 \\ \hline \end{array}$

9. $\begin{array}{r} 8 \\ \times\ 1 \\ \hline \end{array}$

10. $\begin{array}{r} 10 \\ \times\ \ 0 \\ \hline \end{array}$

11. $\begin{array}{r} 1 \\ \times\ 2 \\ \hline \end{array}$

12. $\begin{array}{r} 0 \\ \times\ 9 \\ \hline \end{array}$

Complete each number sentence. Write $<$, $>$, or $=$ for each $\bigcirc$.

13. $8 \times 2 \bigcirc 4 \times 4$

14. $19 \times 1 \bigcirc 37 \times 0$

15. $7 \times 2 \bigcirc 13 + 1$

Complete each number sentence. Write $\times$ or $+$ for each $\bigcirc$.

16. $5 \bigcirc 0 = 5$

17. $5 \bigcirc 1 = 6$

18. $1 \bigcirc 5 = 5$

19. Write a Problem Write a multiplication sentence that shows the Zero Property of Multiplication. Explain why it shows this property.

Name _____

Multiplying with 0 and 1

Find each product.

1. 1×4 **2.** 0×5 **3.** 6×1 **4.** 0×3 **5.** 5×1

_____   _____   _____   _____   _____

6. $\begin{array}{r} 1 \\ \times 1 \\ \hline \end{array}$ **7.** $\begin{array}{r} 0 \\ \times 9 \\ \hline \end{array}$ **8.** $\begin{array}{r} 1 \\ \times 8 \\ \hline \end{array}$ **9.** $\begin{array}{r} 6 \\ \times 1 \\ \hline \end{array}$ **10.** $\begin{array}{r} 7 \\ \times 0 \\ \hline \end{array}$

11. Multiply 1 and 7. _____   **12.** Find 0 times 8. _____

Complete. Write $<$, $>$, or $=$ for each ◯.

13. 1×6 ◯ 3×0 **14.** 5×0 ◯ 1×7 **15.** 1×3 ◯ 3×1

Complete. Write $\times$, $+$, or $-$ for each ☐.

16. $1 \boxed{} 7 = 7$ **17.** $8 \boxed{} 0 = 8$ **18.** $6 \boxed{} 1 = 5$

19. Sara keeps 4 boxes under her bed. Each box is for holding a different type of seashell. There are 0 shells in each box. Write a multiplication sentence to show how many shells Sara has in all.

_____

20. **Communicate** Is the product of 0×0 the same as the sum of $0 + 0$? Explain.

_____

_____

21. A pentagon has 5 sides. Lonnie has a table shaped like a pentagon. How many chairs does Lonnie need if he wants 1 chair on each side?

_____

22. Which multiplication problem below has the greatest product?

    A 5×1 **B** 6×0 **C** 0×7 **D** 8×0

Patterns for Facts

Pattern	Example
All multiples of 2 are even numbers.	2, 8, 16
All multiples of 5 end in 0 or 5.	5, 10, 15
For all multiples of 9, the sum of the digits is always a multiple of 9.	27 $2 + 7 = 9$ 63 $6 + 3 = 9$

1.   9
$\times\ 5$

2.   2
$\times\ 8$

3.   5
$\times\ 8$

4.   9
$\times\ 4$

5.   9
$\times\ 3$

6.   2
$\times\ 7$

7.   5
$\times\ 3$

8.   5
$\times\ 6$

9.   9
$\times\ 2$

10.   5
$\times\ 7$

11.   9
$\times\ 6$

12.   2
$\times\ 6$

13. How many baseball cards are in 3 packages?

_____

14. How many stickers do you get if you buy 7 packages?

Item	Number in Package
Baseball cards	9
Stickers	2
Coupons	5

_____

15. How many coupons do you get if you buy 7 packages?

_____

Patterns for Facts

1.   5
  $\times\ 4$

2.   2
  $\times\ 3$

3.   9
  $\times\ 5$

4.   5
  $\times\ 8$

5.   7
  $\times\ 2$

6.   5
  $\times\ 3$

7.   9
  $\times\ 3$

8.   5
  $\times\ 7$

9. $9 \times 6 =$ _____

10. $2 \times 6 =$ _____

11. $5 \times 5 =$ _____

Find the missing number.

12. _____ $\times\ 9 = 63$

13. $2 \times$ _____ $= 16$

14. A package of baseball cards includes 5 cards. How many baseball cards are in 6 packages?

_____

15. What is the value of the missing number?
$9 \times \boxed{} = 36$

A 6   **B** 4   **C** 3   **D** 2

16. **Writing to Explain** Chris needs to find the product of two numbers. One of the numbers is 6. The answer also needs to be 6. How will he solve this problem? Explain.

_____

_____

_____

10 as a Factor

The table shows the multiplication facts for 10.

10s Facts	
$10 \times 0 = 0$	$10 \times 5 = 50$
$10 \times 1 = 10$	$10 \times 6 = 60$
$10 \times 2 = 20$	$10 \times 7 = 70$
$10 \times 3 = 30$	$10 \times 8 = 80$
$10 \times 4 = 40$	$10 \times 9 = 90$

All multiples of 10 end with zero.

Find 10×5.

To find the answer, you can skip count or you can
write a zero after the 5.

or

Tens	Ones
	5

$\times 10 =$

Tens	Ones
5	0

$5 \times 10 = 50$

---

1. $10 \times 2 =$ _____   **2.** $5 \times 10 =$ _____   **3.** $10 \times 8 =$ _____

4. $2 \times 8 =$ _____   **5.** $\$10 \times 6 =$ _____   **6.** $7 \times 5 =$ _____

7. $\$10 \times 4 =$ _____   **8.** $9 \times 2 =$ _____   **9.** $8 \times 9 =$ _____

10.
$$\begin{array}{r} 10 \\ \times\ \ 3 \\ \hline \end{array}$$

11.
$$\begin{array}{r} \$4 \\ \times\ \ 5 \\ \hline \end{array}$$

12.
$$\begin{array}{r} 2 \\ \times\ \ 2 \\ \hline \end{array}$$

13.
$$\begin{array}{r} \$10 \\ \times\ \ 5 \\ \hline \end{array}$$

14.
$$\begin{array}{r} \$8 \\ \times\ \ 5 \\ \hline \end{array}$$

15.
$$\begin{array}{r} 10 \\ \times\ \ 4 \\ \hline \end{array}$$

16. Reason When you multiply a whole number by 10, what is
always true about the ones place in the product?

_____

10 as a Factor

Find each product.

1. 3×10 **2.** 7×10 **3.** 10×5 **4.** 7×5 **5.** 10×8

_____   _____   _____   _____   _____

6. 9×10 **7.** 6×1 **8.** 10×2 **9.** 9×7 **10.** 4×10

_____   _____   _____   _____   _____

11. 1×10 **12.** 6×10 **13.** 5×4 **14.** 10×10 **15.** 10×3

_____   _____   _____   _____   _____

16. $\begin{array}{r} 8 \\ \times 5 \\ \hline \end{array}$ **17.** $\begin{array}{r} 10 \\ \times 9 \\ \hline \end{array}$ **18.** $\begin{array}{r} 10 \\ \times 8 \\ \hline \end{array}$ **19.** $\begin{array}{r} 10 \\ \times 4 \\ \hline \end{array}$ **20.** $\begin{array}{r} 10 \\ \times 7 \\ \hline \end{array}$

21. $\begin{array}{r} 10 \\ \times 6 \\ \hline \end{array}$ **22.** $\begin{array}{r} 5 \\ \times 2 \\ \hline \end{array}$ **23.** $\begin{array}{r} 10 \\ \times 1 \\ \hline \end{array}$ **24.** $\begin{array}{r} 10 \\ \times 5 \\ \hline \end{array}$ **25.** $\begin{array}{r} 9 \\ \times 0 \\ \hline \end{array}$

26. Mary Ann earns $10 each day walking the neighborhood dogs. How much will she earn in 7 days?

_____

27. A game of basketball requires 10 players. At the park, there are 5 games being played. How many total players are at the park?

_____

28. Mr. Keyes made 4 rows of 10 cookies. Seven of the cookies in the first row were eaten. How many cookies remain?

_____

29. Which is **NOT** a multiple of 10?

A 30

B 55

C 70

D 90

Multiplying by Multiples of 10

You can use basic facts to help you multiply by numbers that are multiples of 10.

$2 \times 7 = 14$ $3 \times 9 = 27$ $5 \times 6 = 30$

$2 \times 70 = 140$ $3 \times 90 = 270$ $5 \times 60 = 300$

To find each of the products above, first complete the basic multiplication fact, then write one zero after the product.
For example:

$9 \times 60 = 540$

First find 9×6. $9 \times 6 = 54$

Then, write one zero
after the product.   540

Find each product.

1. $2 \times 60 =$ _____   **2.** $9 \times 20 =$ _____

3. $5 \times 80 =$ _____   **4.** $2 \times 20 =$ _____

5. $70 \times 3 =$ _____   **6.** $50 \times 6 =$ _____

7. $30 \times 5 =$ _____   **8.** $9 \times 50 =$ _____

9. $7 \times 90 =$ _____   **10.** $7 \times 50 =$ _____

11. Generalize To find 5×40, multiply 5 and 4, then write _____ zero to form the product.

Multiplying by Multiples of 10

Find each product. Use mental math.

1. $5 \times 70 =$ _____

2. $80 \times 5 =$ _____

3. $40 \times 9 =$ _____

4. $20 \times 7 =$ _____

5. $2 \times 60 =$ _____

6. $9 \times 70 =$ _____

7. $8 \times 90 =$ _____

8. $60 \times 9 =$ _____

9. $50 \times 7 =$ _____

10. $80 \times 2 =$ _____

11. How many zeros will the product of 5×60 have?

_____

Mr. Garcia has 30 times as many pencils as Emma. The whole
third grade class has 50 times as many pencils as Emma. Emma has
5 pencils. Use this information for **12** and **13**.

12. How many pencils does
Mr. Garcia have?

13. How many pencils does the
whole third grade class have?

_____   _____

14. Find 3×60.

A 18　　　　　**B** 90　　　　　**C** 180　　　　　**D** 1800

15. **Writing to Explain** Amanda says that the product of 5×40
will have 1 zero. Is she correct? Explain.

_____

_____

_____

Problem Solving:
Two-Question Problems

Sometimes you need the answer to one question to help you answer another question.

Ms. Williams bought 3 pizzas for $8 each. She gave the cashier $30. How much change did she receive?

First, find the cost of the pizzas.

```
_____ in all
| $8 | $8 | $8 |
```

$8 \times 3 = $24

The pizzas cost $24.

Next, find the change.

```
$30 in all
| $24 | ___ |
```

$30 - $24 = $6

Ms. Williams received $6 in change.

1a. Ray bought a pair of sunglasses for $22 and a hat for $19. How much money did the items cost?

```
_____ in all
| $22 | $19 |
```

1b. Ray gave the cashier a $50 bill. How much change should Ray receive?

```
$50 in all
| $41 | ___ |
```

2. Communicate Cindy bought 4 lunch specials for $7 each. She gave the cashier $40. How much change should Cindy receive? Explain how you found your answer.

_____

_____

_____

_____

Problem Solving:
Two-Question Problems

Use the answer from the first problem to solve the second problem.

1a. Lynette bought a book for $13 and a DVD for $22. How much money did the items cost?

```
 _____ in all
| $22    |   $13    |
```

1b. Suppose Lynette paid the cashier with a $50 bill. How much change should Lynette get?

```
    $50 in all
| $35   |  _____  |
```

2a. Melissa bought 2 T-shirts for $9 each. How much money did Melissa spend on T-shirts?

_____

2b. Melissa had $32 in her purse. How much money does she have left?

_____

3a. Curt bought 3 tickets to the movies for $8 each. How much money did Curt spend on movie tickets?

_____

3b. Curt also bought a large popcorn for $5. How much money did Curt spend in all?

_____

4. Lenny bought 4 packs of baseball cards for $3 each. He paid the cashier with a $20 bill. How much change will Lenny receive?

A $7   C $12

B $8   D $13

5. **Write a Problem** Write two problems that can be solved by using the answer from the first problem to solve the second problem.

_____

_____

_____

The Distributive Property

With the Distributive Property, you can break apart a
multiplication fact into the sum of two other facts.

The array below shows
6 × 4 or 6 rows of
4 circles.

6 × 4

You can draw a line to break apart
6 rows of 4 circles into **2** rows of
4 circles *and* **4** rows of 4 circles.

The new facts that stand for the two smaller arrays are
(2 × 4) and (4 × 4).

You can write a number sentence to show this relationship:
6 × 4 = (2 × 4) + (4 × 4).

Draw a line to separate each array into two smaller arrays.
Write the new facts.

1.

2.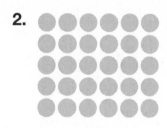

(_____ × _____) and (_____ × _____)   (_____ × _____) and (_____ × _____)

3. Model Don breaks a 4 × 7 array into a 2 × 7 array and another array.
What is the fact for Don's second array? Write a number sentence that
models the relationship of the 4 × 7 array to the other two arrays.

_____

_____

Name _____

The Distributive Property

Draw a line to separate each array into two smaller arrays.
Write the new facts.

1.

2.

(____ × ____) and (____ × ____)   (____ × ____) and (____ × ____)

Use the smaller arrays and the Distributive Property to find
each missing factor. You may use counters to help.

3.

8 × 3 =

(2 × ____) + (____ × 3)

4.

7 × ____ =

(____ × 7) and (____ × ____)

5. Tony broke a larger array into a
2 × 9 array and a 4 × 9 array. What
did the larger array look like? Draw
a picture. Write a number sentence
to show the relationship between
the larger array and the two smaller
arrays.

6. **Use Structure** Which number
makes this number sentence true?

7 × 5 = (■ × 5) + (2 × 5)

A 2   **B** 3

C 4   **D** 5

3 as a Factor

You can use an array to show 3s facts.

3s Facts

$3 \times 0 = 0$	$3 \times 5 = 15$
$3 \times 1 = 3$	$3 \times 6 = 18$
$3 \times 2 = 6$	$3 \times 7 = 21$
$3 \times 3 = 9$	$3 \times 8 = 24$
$3 \times 4 = 12$	$3 \times 9 = 27$

Multiply 2×3 using arrays.

$2 \times 3 = 6$

You can also use a 2s and a 1s fact to find a 3s fact.

Find 7×3.

a. Find a 2s fact with 7: $2 \times 7 = 14$

b. Find a 1s fact with 7: $1 \times 7 = 7$

c. Add the facts: $14 + 7 = 21$

Find each product.

1. 3×2 **2.** 3×4 **3.** 3×5 **4.** 3×1 **5.** 3×9

_____   _____   _____   _____   _____

6. 6×9 **7.** 7×3 **8.** 0×3 **9.** 8×5 **10.** 3×3

_____   _____   _____   _____   _____

11. Reason How can you use a 2s fact and a 1s fact to find 3×8?

_____

_____

Name _____

3 as a Factor

Find the product.

1. 1×3 **2.** 3×7 **3.** 6×3 **4.** 8×3 **5.** 10×5

_____   _____   _____   _____   _____

6. 3×2 **7.** 4×3 **8.** 3×0 **9.** 2×7 **10.** 3×3

_____   _____   _____   _____   _____

11. $\begin{array}{r} 5 \\ \times\ 3 \\ \hline \end{array}$
12. $\begin{array}{r} 10 \\ \times\ 3 \\ \hline \end{array}$
13. $\begin{array}{r} 2 \\ \times\ 3 \\ \hline \end{array}$
14. $\begin{array}{r} 3 \\ \times\ 9 \\ \hline \end{array}$
15. $\begin{array}{r} 9 \\ \times\ 3 \\ \hline \end{array}$

16. A bicycle store also sells tricycles. It has 6 tricycles in stock. How many wheels do the tricycles have in all?

_____

17. There were 5 people who bought tickets to a football game. They bought 3 tickets each. How many tickets were bought in all?

_____

18. **Model** What addition sentence is equal to 4×3?

_____

19. How many small squares are in the figure below?

_____

20. **Construct Arguments** Maria said $7 \times 3 = 21$. Connie said $3 \times 7 = 21$. Who is correct? Explain.

_____

_____

_____

21. Which number is a multiple of 3?

A 16   **B** 20   **C** 24   **D** 28

4 as a Factor

If you know a 2s multiplication fact, you can find a 4s multiplication fact.

4s Facts

4 × 0 = 0	4 × 5 = 20
4 × 1 = 4	4 × 6 = 24
4 × 2 = 8	4 × 7 = 28
4 × 3 = 12	4 × 8 = 32
4 × 4 = 16	4 × 9 = 36

You can double a 2s fact or add a 2s fact by itself to find a 4s fact.

When you double an array of 2 × 1, you get an array of 4 × 1.

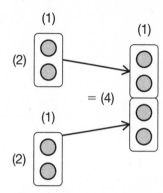

Find 4 × 3 by doubling a 2s fact.

a. Find a 2s fact with 3 as a factor.

  2 × 3 = 6

b. Double it.

  2 × 6 = 12

Find 4 × 3 by adding a 2s fact by itself.

a. Find a 2s fact with 3 as a factor.

  2 × 3 = 6

b. Add the fact to itself.

  6 + 6 = 12

Find each product.

1. 4 × 6   **2.** 8 × 4   **3.** 4 × 5   **4.** 9 × 4   **5.** 4 × 1

_____   _____   _____   _____   _____

6. 4 × 3   **7.** 4 × 7   **8.** 12 × 2   **9.** 0 × 4   **10.** 4 × 4

_____   _____   _____   _____   _____

11. Reason How can you use 2 × 8 to find 4 × 8?

_____

_____

Name _____

4 as a Factor

Find the product.

1. 2×4　　**2.** 4×5　　**3.** 3×4　　**4.** 4×4　　**5.** 5×8

_____　_____　_____　_____　_____

6. 4×6　　**7.** 1×4　　**8.** 4×3　　**9.** 0×4　　**10.** 4×7

_____　_____　_____　_____　_____

11. $\begin{array}{r} 10 \\ \times\ 4 \\ \hline \end{array}$　　**12.** $\begin{array}{r} 1 \\ \times\ 4 \\ \hline \end{array}$　　**13.** $\begin{array}{r} 2 \\ \times\ 4 \\ \hline \end{array}$　　**14.** $\begin{array}{r} 4 \\ \times\ 9 \\ \hline \end{array}$　　**15.** $\begin{array}{r} 8 \\ \times\ 4 \\ \hline \end{array}$

16. What multiplication fact can you double to find 4×7?

_____

17. Each square table can seat 4 people. How many people can be seated at 8 square tables?

_____

18. Jillian sold 4 books of raffle tickets. Each book had 9 tickets. How many tickets did Jillian sell in all?

_____

19. The soccer team has practice 4 times each week during the season. If the season is 10 weeks long, how many practices does the team have?

_____

20. **Writing to Explain** If you know that $4 \times 5 = 20$, how can you use the Commutative (Order) Property of Multiplication to find 5×4?

_____

_____

_____

21. Aaron changed the tires on 5 cars. Each car had 4 tires. How many tires did Aaron change?

A 12　　　　**B** 16　　　　**C** 20　　　　**D** 24

6 and 7 as Factors

You can use multiplication facts that you already know to find other multiplication facts.

You can use a 3s fact to find a 6s fact. Find the 3s fact and then add the product to itself.

Find 6×9.

a. Find the 3s fact with 9: $3 \times 9 = 27$.

b. Add the product to itself: $27 + 27 = 54$.

You can use a 2s and a 5s fact to find a 7s fact.

Find 7×5.

a. Find the 2s fact with 5: $2 \times 5 = 10$.

b. Find the 5s fact with 5: $5 \times 5 = 25$.

c. Add the products: $10 + 25 = 35$.

Find each product.

1. 2×7 **2.** 6×7 **3.** 7×9 **4.** 6×4 **5.** 6×8

_____   _____   _____   _____   _____

6. 7×7 **7.** 6×2 **8.** 8×7 **9.** 3×7 **10.** 6×6

_____   _____   _____   _____   _____

11. $\begin{array}{r} 5 \\ \times\ 6 \\ \hline \end{array}$ **12.** $\begin{array}{r} 7 \\ \times\ 4 \\ \hline \end{array}$ **13.** $\begin{array}{r} 6 \\ \times\ 9 \\ \hline \end{array}$ **14.** $\begin{array}{r} 7 \\ \times\ 3 \\ \hline \end{array}$ **15.** $\begin{array}{r} 7 \\ \times\ 6 \\ \hline \end{array}$

16. Construct Arguments Harold says, "To find 6×8, I can use the facts for 5×4 and 1×4." Do you agree? Explain.

_____

_____

Name _____

6 and 7 as Factors

Find the product. You may draw pictures to help.

1. 5 × 6　　**2.** 6 × 3　　**3.** 6 × 8　　**4.** 3 × 7　　**5.** 7 × 10

_____　　_____　　_____　　_____　　_____

6. 7 × 4　　**7.** 6 × 4　　**8.** 5 × 7　　**9.** 7 × 8　　**10.** 6 × 6

_____　　_____　　_____　　_____　　_____

11.　 7
　　× 6
　　____
12.　 10
　　× 6
　　____
13.　 10
　　× 7
　　____
14.　 7
　　× 7
　　____
15.　 2
　　× 6
　　____

16. Reason What multiplication fact can be found by using the arrays for 2 × 9 and 5 × 9?

_____

17. The chicken eggs that Raul's science class is watching take 3 weeks to hatch. There are 7 days in each week. How many days will it be until the eggs hatch?

_____

18. Emily has 7 apples. She cut each apple into 6 slices. How many slices in all does she have?

_____

19. At a picnic there are 6 tables set up. Each table can seat 8 people. How many people can be seated at the tables in all?

_____

20. How could you use 5 × 6 = 30 to find the product 6 × 6?

_____

_____

_____

21. Barry takes 7 minutes to ride his bicycle one mile. At this rate, how long would Barry take to ride his bicycle 4 miles?

A 21 minutes　　**B** 24 minutes　　**C** 27 minutes　　**D** 28 minutes

Name _____

8 as a Factor

You can double a 4s fact to multiply with 8.

8s Facts

8 × 0 = 0	8 × 5 = 40
8 × 1 = 8	8 × 6 = 48
8 × 2 = 16	8 × 7 = 56
8 × 3 = 24	8 × 8 = 64
8 × 4 = 32	8 × 9 = 72

Find 8 × 6.

a. Find 4 × 6 = 24.

b. Add the product to itself: 24 + 24 = 48

4 × 6 = 24

24 + 24 = 48

4 × 6 = 24

So, 8 × 6 = 48.

Find each product.

1. 2 × 8　　**2.** 4 × 8　　**3.** 8 × 5　　**4.** 7 × 8　　**5.** 8 × 8

_____　　_____　　_____　　_____　　_____

6. 0 × 8　　**7.** 6 × 7　　**8.** 9 × 8　　**9.** 1 × 8　　**10.** 6 × 8

_____　　_____　　_____　　_____　　_____

11. A gallon is equal to 8 pints. How many pints are in 5 gallons?

_____

12. **Writing to Explain** How can you use 4s facts to find 7 × 8?
Give the product in your explanation.

_____

_____

Name _____

8 as a Factor

Find the product.

1. 1×8 **2.** 8×0 **3.** 4×6 **4.** 2×8 **5.** 8×7

_____   _____   _____   _____   _____

6. 8×3 **7.** 4×8 **8.** 8×9 **9.** 8×5 **10.** 8×8

_____   _____   _____   _____   _____

11. $\begin{array}{r} 10 \\ \times\ 8 \\ \hline \end{array}$ **12.** $\begin{array}{r} 7 \\ \times\ 8 \\ \hline \end{array}$ **13.** $\begin{array}{r} 7 \\ \times\ 6 \\ \hline \end{array}$ **14.** $\begin{array}{r} 8 \\ \times\ 3 \\ \hline \end{array}$ **15.** $\begin{array}{r} 9 \\ \times\ 8 \\ \hline \end{array}$

16. An octopus has 8 arms. At the zoo, there are 3 octopuses in one tank. How many arms do the octopuses have in all? _____

17. **Reason** How can you use 4×7 to find 8×7? Find the product.

_____

_____

18. **Construct Arguments** Jose said all of the multiples of 8 are also multiples of 2. Jamila said that all of the multiples of 8 are also multiples of 4. Who is correct? Explain.

_____

_____

19. A package of fruit juice contains 8 boxes. How many boxes are there in 5 packages? _____

20. What is the next number in the pattern below?
16, 24, 32, 40, 48 _____

21. Each package of rolls contains 8 rolls. Ted bought 6 packages. How many rolls did he buy in all?

  A 42   **B** 48   **C** 49   **D** 54

Multiplication Facts

You can use different strategies to multiply.

Find 6×4.

One Way	**Another Way**

One Way

Use a pattern.

6×4 means 6 groups of 4.

So, you can count by 4s.

$6 \times 4 = 24$

Another Way

Use facts you already know.

Use 3s facts to help.

$$6 \times 4 \begin{cases} 3 \times 4 & 3 \times 4 = 12 \\ 3 \times 4 & 3 \times 4 = 12 \end{cases}$$

Add the products.

$12 + 12 = 24$

$6 \times 4 = 24$

In **1** and **2**, use a pattern to find the product.

1. $7 \times 2 =$ _____
Write the numbers you count.

_____ _____ _____ _____

_____ _____ _____

2. $8 \times 5 =$ _____
Write the numbers you count.

_____ _____ _____ _____

_____ _____ _____

In **3–5**, use known facts to find the product. List the facts you used.

3. $6 \times 8 =$ _____

_____

_____

4. $9 \times 5 =$ _____

_____

_____

5. $7 \times 6 =$ _____

_____

_____

6. Writing to Explain Show how to use known facts to find 6×9. Explain how you chose the facts you did.

_____

_____

Multiplication Facts

Find the product.

1. 8×2 **2.** 5×4 **3.** 4×9 **4.** 7×7 **5.** 9×8

_____   _____   _____   _____   _____

6. 2×6 **7.** 1×3 **8.** 5×7 **9.** 4×8 **10.** 6×9

_____   _____   _____   _____   _____

11. $\begin{array}{r} 5 \\ \times\ 4 \\ \hline \end{array}$ **12.** $\begin{array}{r} 1 \\ \times\ 0 \\ \hline \end{array}$ **13.** $\begin{array}{r} 9 \\ \times\ 9 \\ \hline \end{array}$ **14.** $\begin{array}{r} 6 \\ \times\ 6 \\ \hline \end{array}$ **15.** $\begin{array}{r} 10 \\ \times\ 8 \\ \hline \end{array}$

In **16** and **17**, use the table. Write a multiplication sentence and solve.

International Space Station

Expedition Number	Number of Crew Members	Expedition Number	Number of Crew Members	Expedition Number	Number of Crew Members
1	3	5	3	9	2
2	3	6	3	10	2
3	3	7	2	11	2
4	3	8	2	12	2

16. How many crew members in all were in Expeditions 1 through 6?

_____

17. How many crew members in all were in Expeditions 7 through 12?

_____

18. Tia counted the campers in 7 cabins. There were 9 campers in each cabin. How many campers were in the 7 cabins?

A 81   **B** 79   **C** 72   **D** 63

19. Construct Arguments Rick says to find 2×5, he can use counting by 5s: 5, 10, 15, 20, 25. Explain what he did wrong.

_____

_____

Multiplying to Find Combinations

You can use pictures, arrays, and multiplication to help find the number of possible combinations.

Choose one piece of fruit and one kind of toast from the menu. How many different combinations are there?

Fruit	Apple	Banana	Orange
Toast	Wheat	White	

Draw all the combinations of each piece of fruit with wheat toast and each piece of fruit with white toast.

There are 2 rows with 3 combinations in each row. There are 6 combinations.

You can multiply.
Write a multiplication sentence.

$2 \times 3 = 6$

In **1** and **2**, find the number of possible combinations. Use objects, pictures, or multiplication.

1. Choose one letter: A, B, or C and one number: 1, 2, or 3.

   _____

2. Choose one tile color: black or white and one paint color: blue, gray, green, or yellow.

   _____

3. **Communicate** Gina wants one kind of yogurt and one kind of topping. She can choose lemon, lime, or vanilla yogurt. For the topping, she can choose berries, granola, nuts, or peaches. Explain how Gina can find the number of possible combinations.

   _____

   _____

Multiplying to Find Combinations

Roy needs to choose one mark and one shape to make a sign.
Show the possible combinations by filling in the array.

1.

How many different combinations
of one mark and one shape are there?

_____

For **2** and **3**, find the number of possible combinations.
Use objects, pictures, or multiplication.

2. Choose one of 5 kinds of juice
and one of 3 glass sizes.   _____

3. Choose one of 7 shirts and
one of 3 pairs of pants.   _____

4. Reason June has 1 coat and
7 scarves. How many combinations
of a coat and a scarf does she have?   _____

5. Ross has 3 ties and 4 shirts. How many possible
combinations of a tie and a shirt does he have?

   A 3   **B** 4   **C** 12   **D** 21

6. Carl has one kind of bread, crunchy peanut butter and smooth
peanut butter, and different flavors of jelly. What information
do you need to find the number of possible combinations of
peanut butter and jelly sandwiches he can make?

_____

Problem Solving:
Multiple-Step Problems

Enzo's puts 3 meatballs in each of its meatball subs. Carlos's uses 2 times as many meatballs for its meatball subs. Mr. Kerwin orders 4 meatball subs from Carlos's. How many meatballs will be in his subs?

Find and solve the hidden question.

How many meatballs does Carlos's put in each meatball sub?

_____ meatballs in a sub

$$3 \times 2 = 6$$

Carlos's puts 6 meatballs in each of its meatball subs.

Use the answer to the hidden question to solve the problem.

_____ meatballs in all

$$6 \times 4 = 24$$

Mr. Kerwin will have 24 meatballs altogether in his 4 meatball subs.

---

1. Meredith bought a book for $8, a magazine for $5, and bottled water for $2. She paid with a $20 bill. How much change should she get?

   Tip: Find the total cost of the three items.

   _____ in all

   $20 in all

$15	?

   _____

2. Sue bought 3 T-shirts for $8 each. She paid with a $50 bill. How much change should she get?

   _____

3. **Writing to Explain** What steps did you take to answer Exercise 2?

   _____

   _____

   _____

   _____

Name _____

Problem Solving:
Multiple-Step Problems

For **1** through **4**, use the pictures.

1. Teri bought 3 boxes of pencils.
   She paid with a $20 bill. How
   much change did she receive?

   Tip First find the cost of the
   pencils.

   Pencils   Pens   Notebook

_____ in all

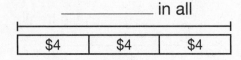

| $4 | $4 | $4 |

$20 in all

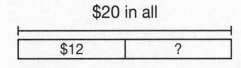

| $12 | ? |

_____

2. Martin bought 3 boxes of pens
   and a calculator. How much
   money did he spend all together?

   Tip First find the cost of the pens.

   _____

3. Joey bought 2 notebooks and
   2 boxes of pencils. How much
   money did he spend all together?

   _____

4. Allie bought 3 notebooks and
   2 boxes of pens. She paid with
   $40. How much change did she
   receive?

   _____

5. **Write a Problem** Write a real-world problem involving multiple steps.
   Then solve your problem.

   _____

   _____

   _____

   _____

6. Bert has $50 in his wallet. Then he buys 2 CDs for $13 each. How much
   money does he have left?

   A $12   **B** $24   **C** $26   **D** $37

Division as Sharing

Division shows how many items are in each group or how many equal groups there are.

There are 15 counters that are going to be put into 5 groups. How many counters will be in each group?

There are 15 counters. There are 5 groups.
There are 3 counters in each group.
So, $15 \div 5 = 3$.

Use counters or draw a picture to solve.

1. 12 tennis balls, 4 cans
How many tennis balls in each can?

_____

2. 20 cookies, 5 bags
How many cookies in each bag?

_____

3. 16 apples, 2 baskets
How many apples in each basket?

_____

4. 20 fingers, 4 hands
How many fingers on each hand?

_____

5. One box contains 12 granola bars. Two bars are in each package.
How many packages are in each box of granola bars?

_____

6. Reason Could you divide 14 shirts into two equal groups?
Why or why not?

_____

_____

Name _____

Division as Sharing

Use counters or draw a picture to solve.

1. 24 people, 4 rows
How many people in each row?

[ ]

_____

2. 18 marbles, 2 people
How many marbles for each person?

[ ]

_____

3. 25 apples, 5 trees
How many apples on each tree?

[ ]

_____

4. 21 books, 3 shelves
How many books on each shelf?

[ ]

_____

Complete each division sentence.

5.

15

$15 \div 3 = \boxed{}$

6.

16

$16 \div 4 = \boxed{}$

7. Explain It Ron and Pam each have 20 pennies. Ron will put his pennies into 4 groups. Pam will put her pennies into 5 groups. Who will have more pennies in each group? Explain.

_____

_____

8. There are 28 days in February. There are 7 days in a week. How many weeks are there in February?

   A 3   **B** 4   **C** 5   **D** 6

Division as Repeated Subtraction

You can think of division as repeated subtraction.

Emily has 20 raffle tickets. There are 5 tickets in each book.
How many books of raffle tickets does Emily have?

Start with 20 tickets. Subtract 5.	$20 - 5 = 15$
Subtract 5 more tickets.	$15 - 5 = 10$
Subtract 5 more tickets.	$10 - 5 = 5$
Subtract 5 more tickets.	$5 - 5 = 0$
You have reached 0.	

You have subtracted 5 four times.
So, $20 \div 5 = 4$.

Emily has 4 books of raffle tickets.

Use counters or draw a picture to solve.

1. 10 markers
   5 markers in each box
   How many boxes?

   _____

2. 8 hamsters
   2 hamsters in each cage
   How many cages?

   _____

3. 16 books
   4 books on each shelf
   How many shelves?

   _____

4. 18 players
   3 players on each team
   How many teams?

   _____

5. Annie had 16 balloons. She shares them equally with Connie.
   How many balloons does each girl have now?

   _____

6. **Communicate** Show how you can use repeated subtraction
   to find how many groups of 7 are in 28.
   Then write the division sentence for the problem.

   _____

   _____

Division as Repeated Subtraction

Use counters or draw a picture to solve.

1. 18 pens
3 pens in each box
How many boxes?

_____

2. 24 students
3 students on each team
How many teams?

_____

3. 35 stickers
5 stickers on each sheet
How many sheets?

_____

4. 30 leaves
6 leaves painted on each vase
How many vases?

_____

5. Number Sense What division
sentence means the same as the
following subtraction sentences?

$12 - 4 = 8$

$8 - 4 = 4$

$4 - 4 = 0$

_____

6. Tandem bicycles are ridden by
2 people. If 14 people rented
tandem bicycles, how many
bicycles were rented?

_____

7. Explain It Tamara says that $15 \div 3 = 5$. Is she correct? Explain.

_____

_____

_____

8. Keisha has to carry 32 boxes to her room. She can carry
4 boxes on each trip. How many trips will she take?

A 6   **B** 7   **C** 8   **D** 9

Writing Division Stories

Eddie was asked to write a division story using 12 ÷ 4.

Eddie wrote his story this way.

Cami has 12 crayons and some cans.
She puts 4 crayons into each can.

How many cans did Cami use?

Think of a situation where the larger number can be put into groups.

Write your question.

You can show Eddie's story this way.

Cami used 3 cans.

Write a division story for each number sentence.
Then use counters or draw a picture to solve.

1. 10 ÷ 2 = ☐

_____

_____

2. 21 ÷ 3 = ☐

_____

_____

3. 18 ÷ 3 = ☐

_____

_____

4. 16 ÷ 4 = ☐

_____

_____

5. Explain It Sheila wrote a division story. She asked how many equal groups 24 flowers could be put into. What information must she give about the groups?

_____

_____

Writing Division Stories

Write a division story for each number sentence.
Then use counters or draw a picture to solve.

1. 54 ÷ 6 = ☐

_____

_____

_____

_____

2. 36 ÷ 9 = ☐

_____

_____

_____

_____

3. 42 ÷ 7 = ☐

_____

_____

_____

4. 25 ÷ 5 = ☐

_____

_____

_____

5. There are 40 relatives at a party. There are 5 tables that each seat the same number of people. How many people can sit at each table?

_____

6. A softball pitcher needs to get 3 outs in an inning. If a pitcher gets 21 outs, how many innings did she pitch?

_____

7. Explain It There are 16 people at a party. They want to set up relay teams with exactly 3 people each. Will each person be on a team? Explain.

_____

_____

Problem Solving: Use Objects and Draw a Picture

Sometimes, drawing a picture will help you solve a problem. It will help you "see" the problem and perhaps the solution.

Some orange juice spilled on a tile floor and covered up part of the floor. The tile floor was in the shape of a rectangle. There were 40 square tiles in the whole floor. How many tiles were in each row?

Draw a picture to show what you know.

You can see how many rows are not covered by juice on the floor.

Finish the picture to solve the problem.

There should be 40 tiles in all.

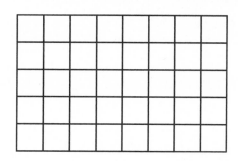

So there are 8 tiles in each row.

Solve. Use objects or draw a picture.

1. Mr. Robbins spilled stain on part of a tiled floor. The whole section of floor was shaped like a rectangle. There were 45 squares in the section. How many squares were in each row?

2. Kate is painting a wall. She painted over part of a section of 30 square tiles. The whole section of tiles was shaped like a rectangle. How many rows of tiles were in the whole section?

Problem Solving: Use Objects and Draw a Picture

Solve. Use objects or draw a picture.

1. Ron painted part of a tiled section of his bathroom floor. The whole section was shaped like a rectangle. There were 35 square tiles in the section. How many tiles were in each row?

_____

2. Some syrup spilled on a checkerboard-style table. The syrup covered some of the tiles. There were 36 squares on the table. How many of the squares had syrup on them?

_____

3. Dress rehearsal of the play was attended by 142 people. Opening night was attended by 238 people. How many people saw the two shows in all?

_____ people in all	
142	238

4. Carol and Deanna drove 320 miles altogether this weekend. They drove 196 miles on Sunday. How many miles did they drive on Saturday?

320 miles in all	
	196

5. Write a Problem Write and solve a real-world problem that you can solve by using objects or drawing a picture.

_____

_____

Relating Multiplication and Division

You can use multiplication facts to understand division.
Fact families show how multiplication and division are related.

Here is the fact family for 3, 8, and 24:

$3 \times 8 = 24$ $24 \div 3 = 8$

$8 \times 3 = 24$ $24 \div 8 = 3$

Complete. Use counters or draw a picture to solve.

1. $3 \times \boxed{} = 6$

     $6 \div 3 = \boxed{}$

2. $7 \times \boxed{} = 14$

     $14 \div 7 = \boxed{}$

3. $5 \times \boxed{} = 20$

     $20 \div 5 = \boxed{}$

4. $4 \times \boxed{} = 24$

     $24 \div 4 = \boxed{}$

5. Reason What other number is a part of this fact family? 3, 4, _____

6. There are 28 days in 4 weeks. What fact family would you use to find the number of days in 1 week?

_____

7. There are 12 inches in 1 foot. What fact family would you use to find the number of inches in 2 feet?

_____

Relating Multiplication and Division

Complete. Use counters or draw a picture to help.

1. $5 \times \boxed{} = 15$

   $15 \div 5 = \boxed{}$

2. $6 \times \boxed{} = 24$

   $24 \div 6 = \boxed{}$

3. $7 \times \boxed{} = 35$

   $35 \div 7 = \boxed{}$

4. $5 \times \boxed{} = 25$

   $25 \div 5 = \boxed{}$

5. $3 \times \boxed{} = 12$

   $12 \div 3 = \boxed{}$

6. $3 \times \boxed{} = 27$

   $27 \div 3 = \boxed{}$

7. Write a fact family for 3, 6, and 18.

   _____

   _____

8. Patrick purchased 12 books. He needed 4 books for each of his projects at school. How many projects did he have?

   _____

9. **Model** Draw an array. Then write a fact family to describe your array.

   _____

   _____

10. **Critique Reasoning** Evan told his class that the people in his family have 14 legs in all. Quinton said that there must be 7 people in Evan's family. Is Quinton correct? Explain.

    _____

    _____

11. Which number makes this number sentence true? $\blacksquare \div 6 = 8$

    A 2   **B** 14   **C** 24   **D** 48

Name _____

Fact Families with 2, 3, 4, and 5

You can use multiplication facts to help you find quotients.

Example 1
Darren and Molly have 16 sheets of paper to share. Each will get the same number of sheets of paper. How many sheets will each get?

Example 2
Peter has 24 pennies. He puts the pennies into 4 equal rows. How many pennies are in each row?

What You Think	What You Write	What You Think	What You Write
2 times what number equals 16? $2 \times 8 = 16$	$16 \div 2 = 8$ Darren and Molly will each get 8 sheets of paper.	4 times what number equals 24? $4 \times 6 = 24$	$24 \div 4 = 6$ Peter has 6 pennies in each row.

Find each quotient.

1. $14 \div 2$ 2. $35 \div 5$ 3. $15 \div 3$ 4. $32 \div 4$ 5. $24 \div 3$

_____   _____   _____   _____   _____

6. $2\overline{)12}$ 7. $3\overline{)27}$ 8. $5\overline{)25}$ 9. $4\overline{)20}$ 10. $4\overline{)36}$

11. Write a fact family using the numbers 5, 6, and 30.

_____

_____

Name _____

Fact Families with 2, 3, 4, and 5

Find each quotient.

1. $14 \div 2$ **2.** $12 \div 3$ **3.** $16 \div 4$ **4.** $30 \div 5$ **5.** $20 \div 2$

_____   _____   _____   _____   _____

6. $3\overline{)21}$ **7.** $4\overline{)32}$ **8.** $5\overline{)40}$ **9.** $3\overline{)18}$ **10.** $5\overline{)45}$

11. Find 18 divided by 3.   **12.** Divide 36 by 4.   **13.** Find 35 divided by 5.

_____   _____   _____

Find each missing number.

14. $27 \div \boxed{} = 3$ **15.** $30 \div 3 = \boxed{}$ **16.** $\boxed{} \div 2 = 7$

Reason Write $<$ or $>$ to compare.

17. $5 \times 2 \bigcirc 8 \div 2$ **18.** $3 \times 6 \bigcirc 6 \div 3$ **19.** $4 + 8 \bigcirc 4 \times 8$

20. Gabriella and 3 friends shared a pack of 12 stickers equally. How many stickers did each person get?

21. Erica counted 45 fingers when the students were asked who wants to play kickball. How many hands went up?

_____   _____

22. Franklin says that if he divides 40 by 5, he will get 8. Jeff says he should get 9. Who is correct? Explain.

_____

_____

23. Which fact does **NOT** belong in the same fact family as $24 \div 4 = 6$?

    A $4 \times 6 = 24$ **B** $6 + 4 = 10$ **C** $24 \div 6 = 4$ **D** $6 \times 4 = 24$

Fact Families with 6 and 7

Multiplication facts can help you to find division facts when
6 or 7 is the divisor.

Find 35 ÷ 7.

There are 48 marbles. They come in
packages of 6. How many packages
of marbles are there?

Find 48 ÷ 6.

What You Think	What You Write	What You Think	What You Write
What number times 7 equals 35? 7 × **5** = 35	35 ÷ 7 = **5**	What number times 6 equals 48? 6 × **8** = 48	48 ÷ 6 = **8** There are 8 packages of marbles.

Find each quotient.

1. 30 ÷ 6   **2.** 28 ÷ 7   **3.** 36 ÷ 6   **4.** 21 ÷ 7   **5.** 42 ÷ 6

_____   _____   _____   _____   _____

6. 7)49   **7.** 6)54   **8.** 7)70   **9.** 6)48   **10.** 7)56

11. Reason Name a number that can be evenly divided by 6 and by 7.

_____

12. Reason Using 6 as one of the numbers, write a fact family
with only two facts.

_____

Fact Families with 6 and 7

Find each quotient.

1. 24 ÷ 6   **2.** 42 ÷ 7   **3.** 36 ÷ 4   **4.** 63 ÷ 7   **5.** 40 ÷ 5

_____   _____   _____   _____   _____

6. 6)48   **7.** 7)49   **8.** 2)12   **9.** 6)36   **10.** 3)27

11. Find 70 divided by 7.   **12.** Divide 66 by 6.   **13.** Find 48 divided by 6.

_____   _____   _____

14. Communicate How can you use a multiplication fact to find a division fact?

_____

_____

15. Sierra's karate class lasts 56 days.
How many weeks does the class last?   _____

16. Critique Reasoning Wendell has a box with 36 cherries. He divides
the cherries equally among 5 friends and himself. Bonnie received
6 cherries. She thinks she should have received one more.
Is she correct? Explain.

_____

_____

_____

17. Mr. Kline brought 30 boxes of fruit juice to a soccer game.
Fruit juice comes in packages of 6. How many packages
did Mr. Kline bring?   _____

18. Katie bought 42 baseball cards. The cards come in packs of 7.
How many packs of cards did Katie buy?

    A 5   **B** 6   **C** 7   **D** 8

Fact Families with 8 and 9

Multiplication facts can help you to find division facts when 8 or 9 is the divisor.

There are 32 counters. There are 8 counters in each row. How many rows are there?	There are 45 counters. There are 9 rows. How many counters are in each row?

What You Think	**What You Write**	**What You Think**	**What You Write**
8 times what number equals 32? 8 × **4** = 32	32 ÷ 8 = **4** There are 4 rows of counters.	9 times what number equals 45? 9 × **5** = 45	45 ÷ 9 = **5** There are 5 counters in each row.

Find each quotient.

1. 54 ÷ 9   **2.** 24 ÷ 8   **3.** 56 ÷ 8   **4.** 36 ÷ 9   **5.** 63 ÷ 9

_____   _____   _____   _____   _____

6. 9)72   **7.** 8)48   **8.** 8)40   **9.** 8)80   **10.** 9)81

11. Reason What multiplication fact could you use to find a number that can be divided evenly by 8 and by 9?

_____

Name _____

8-4

Fact Families with 8 and 9

Find each quotient.

1. $48 \div 8$ **2.** $18 \div 9$ **3.** $49 \div 7$ **4.** $64 \div 8$ **5.** $45 \div 9$

_____   _____   _____   _____   _____

6. $6\overline{)42}$ **7.** $8\overline{)72}$ **8.** $9\overline{)36}$ **9.** $5\overline{)15}$ **10.** $8\overline{)56}$

11. Find 81 divided by 9.   **12.** Divide 40 by 8.   **13.** Find 90 divided by 9.

_____   _____   _____

Write $<$ or $>$ to compare.

14. $63 \div 9 \bigcirc 8$ **15.** $32 \div 8 \bigcirc 8$ **16.** $54 \div 9 \bigcirc 5$

17. Reason It costs $7 for a matinee and $8 for an evening movie. With $56, would you be able to buy more matinee tickets or evening tickets? Explain.

_____

_____

18. Teri scored 64 points in the first 8 basketball games she played in. She scored the same number of points in each game. How many points did she score in each game? _____

19. Communicate Adam made 19 paper cranes Monday and 8 more Tuesday. He gave 9 friends an equal number of cranes. How many cranes did each friend receive? Explain how you found your answer.

_____

_____

_____

20. A short story consists of 81 pages. Andrea will read 9 pages each day. How many days will it take Andrea to finish the story?

     A 6   **B** 7   **C** 8   **D** 9

Copyright © Pearson Education, Inc., or its affiliates. All Rights Reserved. 3

Multiplication and Division Facts

A class is making popcorn for a carnival. Each batch makes
30 cups. They put the popcorn in bags that hold 6 cups each.
How many bags of popcorn does one batch make?

You can solve the problem using division or multiplication.

Division	**Multiplication**
How many groups of 6 are in 30?	What number times 6 equals 30?

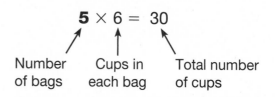

Divide the total number of cups by
the number of cups in each bag:
$30 \div 6 = \mathbf{5}$ ← Number of bags

Each batch of popcorn makes 5 bags.

Complete the equations.

1. $21 \div 3 = \boxed{}$

$3 \times \boxed{} = 21$

2. $36 \div 6 = \boxed{}$

$6 \times \boxed{} = 36$

3. $18 \div 9 = \boxed{}$

$9 \times \boxed{} = 18$

4. $54 \div 9 = \boxed{}$

$9 \times \boxed{} = 54$

5. There are 24 students running in a relay race. Each relay
team needs 4 students. How many teams will they make?
Write a division sentence and a multiplication sentence.

_____   _____

6. Writing to Explain The same number makes both of these
equations true. What number is it? Explain.

$56 \div 8 = \blacksquare$ $8 \times \blacksquare = 56$

_____

_____

Name _____

Multiplication and Division Facts

Complete the number sentences.

1. $35 \div 5 = \boxed{}$ **2.** $27 \div \boxed{} = 3$ **3.** $42 \div 7 = \boxed{}$ **4.** $32 \div \boxed{} = 4$

$\boxed{} \times 5 = 35$ $3 \times \boxed{} = 27$ $\boxed{} \times 7 = 42$ $4 \times \boxed{} = 32$

Find each product or quotient.

5. $16 \div 4$ **6.** 9×7 **7.** $30 \div 5$ **8.** 8×3 **9.** 4×9

_____   _____   _____   _____   _____

10. $25 \div 5$ **11.** $45 \div 9$ **12.** 8×8 **13.** 7×4 **14.** $54 \div 6$

_____   _____   _____   _____   _____

15. Find 36 divided by 6.   **16.** Multiply 8 and 9.   **17.** Divide 48 by 8.

_____   _____   _____

18. A music store has 5 guitars for sale. Each guitar has 6 strings. The manager wants to replace all the strings. How many new strings does he need?

   A 6
   B 18
   C 24
   D 30

19. Tolen has 18 dog treats. He gives the same number of treats to the 6 dogs at the pet store where he works. Which equation can be used to find the number of treats each dog gets?

   A $18 + 6 = 24$
   B $18 \div 6 = 3$
   C $18 - 6 = 12$
   D $18 \div 18 = 1$

20. Communicate Jason has 3 bags with 5 mangos in each bag. Maria has 5 bags with 4 mangos in each bag. Explain how you can tell who has more without finding the total number of mangos each person has.

_____

_____

Problem Solving: Draw a Picture and Write a Number Sentence

You can draw a picture to help you divide.

Neil has 54 CDs. He has the CDs equally placed among 6 shelves. How many CDs can go on each shelf?

Draw a diagram to show the problem. Make 6 rows with the same number of CDs until you reach 54.

Write a number sentence: $54 \div 6 = 9$.

Check your answer by using multiplication: $6 \times 9 = 54$.

Neil can put 9 CDs on each shelf.

Draw a diagram to show what you know.
Then write a number sentence and solve.

1. There are 5 cars taking students to a museum. Each car can seat 4 students. How many students can go to the museum?

2. There are 16 players competing in the beach volleyball tournament. There are 8 teams competing. How many players are on each team?

_____   _____

3. **Communicate** Sandy said she could use addition to answer question 1. How could this be done?

_____

_____

Name _____

Problem Solving: Draw a Picture and Write a Number Sentence

In **1** and **2**, draw a diagram to show what you know.
Then write a number sentence and solve.

1. Maria bought 5 cans of tennis balls. Each can contained 3 tennis balls. How many tennis balls did Maria buy altogether?

2. In Ms. Ramirez's class, there are 28 students. They sit in 4 equal rows. How many students are in each row?

_____

_____

In **3** and **4**, use the chart.

3. A community center has 3 tennis teams and 5 basketball teams. No one is on both teams. How many athletes are there?

Players on Team	
Sport	**Players**
Tennis	2
Basketball	5
Softball	10

_____

4. **Critique Reasoning** Fabio said that there are 3 times as many people on a basketball team as on a tennis team. Is he correct? Explain.

_____

_____

_____

Write a number sentence and solve. Use this information for **5** and **6**.

Marshall sleeps 8 hours each day.

5. How many hours does Marshall sleep in one week? _____

6. How many hours is Marshall awake each day? _____

7. Tricia spent $12 to rent ice skates. She rented them for 4 hours. Which number sentence can you write to find how much it costs to rent skates for one hour?

   A $12 − 4 = ∎ B $12 + 4 = ∎ C $12 × 4 = ∎ D $12 ÷ 4 = ∎

Dividing Regions into Equal Parts

A whole can be divided into equal parts in different ways.

| 2 equal parts **halves** | 3 equal parts **thirds** | 4 equal parts **fourths** | 5 equal parts **fifths** |

| 6 equal parts **sixths** | 8 equal parts **eighths** | 10 equal parts **tenths** | 12 equal parts **twelfths** |

Tell if each shows equal parts or unequal parts.
If the parts are equal, name them.

1.

2.

3.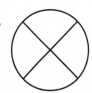

_____   _____   _____

Name the equal parts of the whole.

4.

5.

6.

_____   _____   _____

7. Using grid paper, draw a picture of a whole that is divided into thirds.

8. **Reason** How many equal parts are there when you divide a figure into fifths? _____

Name _____

Dividing Regions into Equal Parts

Tell if each shows equal or unequal parts.
If the parts are equal, name them.

1.

_____

_____

2.

_____

_____

3.

_____

_____

4.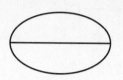

_____

_____

Name the equal parts of the whole.

5.

_____

6.

_____

7.

_____

8.

_____

Use the grid to draw a region showing the number of equal parts
named.

9. eighths

10. sixths

11. How many equal parts does this figure have?

_____

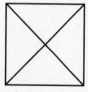

12. Which is the name of 12 equal parts of a whole?

   A halves   **B** sixths   **C** tenths   **D** twelfths

Fraction Number Lines

The distance between fractions with the same denominator on a number line is exactly the same.

You can make the fractions closer together or farther apart. The fractions in the number line below are closer together than the fractions in the number line above.

Both number lines show the same fractions.

Write the value of *A* and *B* for each number line.

1.

_____

2.

_____

3. Reason Which letter on this number line has the lesser value: *A* or *B*? Explain your answer.

_____

_____

_____

Understanding Number Lines

Write the value of *A*, *B*, and *C* on each number line.

1.

2.

3.

4. Critique Reasoning Lara said that point *D* has a value of $\frac{6}{8}$. Is her statement reasonable? Explain your answer.

_____

_____

5. Which point represents $\frac{1}{2}$ on this number line?

     A point *E*   **B** point *F*   **C** point *G*   **D** point *H*

Locating Fractions on the Number Line

Number lines can be used to show fractions. In the number lines below, the denominator shows the number of equally sized sections between 0 and 1.

| 0 | $\frac{1}{4}$ | $\frac{2}{4}$ | $\frac{3}{4}$ | 1 |

| 0 | $\frac{1}{6}$ | $\frac{2}{6}$ | $\frac{3}{6}$ | $\frac{4}{6}$ | $\frac{5}{6}$ | 1 |

This number line is divided into fourths.

This number line is divided into sixths.

Number lines can also represent mixed numbers.

| 0 | $\frac{1}{2}$ | 1 | $1\frac{1}{2}$ | 2 | $2\frac{1}{2}$ | 3 | $3\frac{1}{2}$ | 4 |

This number line is divided into halves.

Write the missing fraction or mixed number for each number line.

1.

0 $\frac{1}{8}$ $\frac{2}{8}$ $\frac{3}{8}$ ☐ ☐ ☐ ☐ 1

2.

0 $\frac{1}{3}$ $\frac{2}{3}$ 1 $1\frac{1}{3}$ ☐ 2 $2\frac{1}{3}$ $2\frac{2}{3}$ 3

3.

0 ☐ $\frac{2}{4}$ ☐ 1 ☐ $1\frac{2}{4}$ ☐ 2 $2\frac{1}{4}$ ☐ ☐ 3

4. Construct Arguments Erica said that $1\frac{3}{4}$ is between 2 and 3 on a number line. Do you agree? Why or why not?

_____

_____

Name _____

Locating Fractions on the Number Line

Write the missing fraction or mixed number for each number line.

1.

2.

The number line below shows how many miles different places are from the pet shop. Use the number line for **3–5**.

3. The park is 4 miles from the pet shop. How far is the mall from the pet shop?

_____

4. Reason Ken lives halfway between the pet shop and the park. How far does Ken live from school?

_____

5. The movie theater is twice as far from the school as the mall. If the movie theater is to the right of the school, at which location is the movie theater?

_____

6. Roberta is going to make a number line from 0 to 4 by $\frac{1}{4}$s. Not including the mark for 0, how many marks should she draw?

    A 8   **B** 12   **C** 16   **D** 20

Name _____

Fractions and Length

A fraction can name part of the length of an object.

What part of this line segment is black?

━━━━━━━━━━━━━━━━━━━━ ━━━ ━━━

You can use fraction strips to find the part of the whole.

━━━━━━━━━━━━ ━━━ ━━━

$\frac{1}{4}$	$\frac{1}{4}$	$\frac{1}{4}$	$\frac{1}{4}$

The line segment is $\frac{3}{4}$ black. The line segment is $\frac{1}{4}$ gray.

What fraction of the length of the 1 strip do the other strips show?

1.

1

$\frac{1}{4}$

_____

2.

_____

3.

1

$\frac{1}{8}$	$\frac{1}{8}$

_____

4.

_____

5. What fraction of the line segment is black?   _____

━━━━━━━━━━━━━━━ ━━━━━

$\frac{1}{8}$	$\frac{1}{8}$	$\frac{1}{8}$	$\frac{1}{8}$	$\frac{1}{8}$	$\frac{1}{8}$	$\frac{1}{8}$	$\frac{1}{8}$

6. Reason A figure is part blue and part red.

It is $\frac{5}{8}$ red. What part of the figure is blue?   _____

Fractions and Length

What fraction of the length of the 1 strip do the other strips show?

1.

1

$\frac{1}{3}$

_____

2.

1

$\frac{1}{4}$	$\frac{1}{4}$	$\frac{1}{4}$

_____

3.

1

$\frac{1}{8}$	$\frac{1}{8}$	$\frac{1}{8}$	$\frac{1}{8}$	$\frac{1}{8}$

_____

4.

1

$\frac{1}{6}$	$\frac{1}{6}$	$\frac{1}{6}$	$\frac{1}{6}$

_____

In **5** and **6**, what fraction of each length of yarn is black?

5.

$\frac{1}{3}$	$\frac{1}{3}$	$\frac{1}{3}$

_____

6.

$\frac{1}{2}$	$\frac{1}{2}$

_____

7. Writing to Explain What is the purpose of using fraction strips and a 1 strip?

_____

_____

_____

_____

8. About $\frac{6}{8}$ of Earth's surface is covered by water. About what fraction of Earth's surface is not covered by water?

A $\frac{5}{8}$

B $\frac{1}{2}$

C $\frac{3}{8}$

D $\frac{2}{8}$

Problem Solving: Writing to Explain

Gina and her brother Don made homemade pasta with their mother. Gina made $\frac{1}{4}$ of a pan of pasta. Don made $\frac{3}{8}$ of a pan. Which person made more pasta?

Writing to Explain

- Write your explanation in steps to make it clear.

- Tell what the numbers mean in your explanation.

- Tell why you took certain steps.

Example

- Because $\frac{1}{4}$ and $\frac{3}{8}$ have different denominators, I multiplied the numerator and denominator of $\frac{1}{4}$ by 2 to get $\frac{2}{8}$.

- Then I could compare the numerators of $\frac{2}{8}$ and $\frac{3}{8}$. Because $\frac{3}{8}$ is greater than $\frac{2}{8}$ I knew that Don made more pasta.

1. Rick has a collection of 6 video games. He lets his best friend borrow $\frac{2}{6}$ of his video game collection. Write two fractions equivalent to this number. Explain how you came up with the fractions.

_____

_____

_____

_____

_____

_____

Problem Solving: Writing to Explain

1. Mary has 12 marbles. $\frac{3}{12}$ of the marbles are yellow and $\frac{2}{12}$ of the marbles are blue. The rest of the marbles are green. How many marbles are green? Explain how you know.

    _____

    _____

    _____

    _____

2. Adam wants to compare the fractions $\frac{3}{12}$, $\frac{1}{6}$, and $\frac{1}{3}$. He wants to order them from least to greatest and rewrite them so they all have the same denominator. Explain how Adam can rewrite the fractions.

    _____

    _____

    _____

    _____

3. Adam used the three fractions to make a circle graph and colored each a different color. What fraction of the graph is not colored? Explain your answer.

    _____

    _____

    _____

Using Models to Compare Fractions: Same Denominator

You can use fraction strips to compare fractions with the same denominator.

Compare $\frac{2}{4}$ and $\frac{3}{4}$.

1		
$\frac{1}{4}$	$\frac{1}{4}$	
$\frac{1}{4}$	$\frac{1}{4}$	$\frac{1}{4}$

$$\frac{2}{4} \bigcirc \frac{3}{4}$$

When fractions have the same denominator, the fraction with the *greater* numerator is greater.

Compare. Write >, <, or =.

1.

1				
$\frac{1}{8}$	$\frac{1}{8}$	$\frac{1}{8}$	$\frac{1}{8}$	
$\frac{1}{8}$	$\frac{1}{8}$	$\frac{1}{8}$	$\frac{1}{8}$	$\frac{1}{8}$

$$\frac{5}{8} \bigcirc \frac{4}{8}$$

2.

$$\frac{1}{4} \bigcirc \frac{3}{4}$$

3. $\frac{5}{6} \bigcirc \frac{2}{6}$

4. $\frac{2}{3} \bigcirc \frac{1}{3}$

5. If two fractions have the same denominator but different numerators, which fraction is greater? Give an example.

_____

_____

_____

Using Models to Compare Fractions: Same Denominator

Compare. Write >, <, or =.

1.

$\frac{3}{6}$ ◯ $\frac{2}{6}$

2.

$\frac{1}{3}$ ◯ $\frac{2}{3}$

3. $\frac{2}{4}$ ◯ $\frac{3}{4}$

4. $\frac{5}{6}$ ◯ $\frac{3}{6}$

5. $\frac{4}{6}$ ◯ $\frac{1}{6}$

6. $\frac{3}{8}$ ◯ $\frac{6}{8}$

7. Why is $\frac{6}{8}$ greater than $\frac{5}{8}$ but less than $\frac{7}{8}$?

_____

_____

_____

_____

8. **Reasonableness** Marty ate $\frac{4}{6}$ of his pizza and Luis ate $\frac{5}{6}$ of his pizza. Marty ate more pizza than Luis. How is that possible?

_____

_____

_____

_____

9. Two fractions have the same denominator. Which is the greater fraction: the fraction with the greater numerator or the lesser numerator?

_____

_____

10. Which is the greatest fraction?

   A $\frac{0}{4}$ **B** $\frac{1}{4}$ **C** $\frac{3}{4}$ **D** $\frac{2}{4}$

Name _____

Using Models to Compare Fractions: Same Numerator

You can compare fractions with the same numerator using fraction strips.

Compare $\frac{1}{3}$ and $\frac{1}{4}$.

$\frac{1}{3}$ ◯ $\frac{1}{4}$

When fractions have the same numerator, the fraction with the *lesser* denominator is greater.

Compare. Write <, >, or =.

1.

$\frac{2}{8}$ ◯ $\frac{2}{6}$

2.

$\frac{3}{4}$ ◯ $\frac{3}{8}$

3. $\frac{2}{3}$ ◯ $\frac{2}{3}$

4. $\frac{3}{4}$ ◯ $\frac{3}{6}$

5. Reason If two fractions have the same numerator but different denominators, which fraction is greater? Give an example.

_____

_____

_____

Using Models to Compare Fractions: Same Numerator

Compare. Write <, >, or = for each ◯.

1.

$\frac{1}{8}$ ◯ $\frac{1}{3}$

2.

$\frac{2}{3}$ ◯ $\frac{2}{6}$

3. $\frac{3}{6}$ ◯ $\frac{3}{4}$

4. $\frac{1}{2}$ ◯ $\frac{1}{2}$

5. $\frac{2}{8}$ ◯ $\frac{2}{6}$

6. $\frac{3}{8}$ ◯ $\frac{3}{4}$

7. Ricardo has read $\frac{2}{3}$ of a book. Lin had read $\frac{2}{4}$ of the same book. Who has read more of the book?

_____

8. Maria and Nina each ordered a small pizza. Maria ate $\frac{3}{8}$ of her pizza. Nina ate $\frac{3}{6}$ of her pizza. Who ate more pizza?

_____

9. Which is the greatest fraction?

A $\frac{1}{2}$ **B** $\frac{1}{4}$ **C** $\frac{1}{6}$ **D** $\frac{1}{8}$

10. Writing to Explain Why is $\frac{1}{6}$ greater than $\frac{1}{8}$ but less than $\frac{1}{3}$? Explain.

_____

_____

Using Fractions

You can use fraction strips or a number line to compare and order fractions and mixed numbers.

Compare $\frac{3}{4}$, $\frac{5}{8}$, and $\frac{1}{2}$. Which fraction is the greatest? the least?

Use fraction strips to compare.

$\frac{1}{4}$	$\frac{1}{4}$	$\frac{1}{4}$	
$\frac{1}{8}$ $\frac{1}{8}$	$\frac{1}{8}$ $\frac{1}{8}$	$\frac{1}{8}$	
$\frac{1}{2}$			

$\frac{3}{4} > \frac{5}{8}$ and $\frac{5}{8} > \frac{1}{2}$

$\frac{3}{4}$ is the greatest.

$\frac{1}{2}$ is the least.

Use a number line to compare.

$\frac{3}{4}$ is to the right of $\frac{5}{8}$ so $\frac{3}{4} > \frac{5}{8}$.

$\frac{5}{8}$ is to the right of $\frac{1}{2}$ so $\frac{5}{8} > \frac{1}{2}$.

$\frac{3}{4}$ is the greatest.

$\frac{1}{2}$ is the least.

In **1–4**, write the fractions in order from least to greatest.

1. $\frac{4}{6}, \frac{3}{8}, \frac{1}{2}$ _____

2. $\frac{5}{6}, \frac{3}{4}, \frac{4}{8}$ _____

3. $\frac{1}{2}, \frac{6}{8}, \frac{2}{6}$ _____

4. $\frac{3}{8}, \frac{1}{2}, \frac{1}{4}$ _____

$\frac{1}{2}$			$\frac{1}{2}$		
$\frac{1}{4}$		$\frac{1}{4}$	$\frac{1}{4}$		$\frac{1}{4}$
$\frac{1}{6}$	$\frac{1}{6}$	$\frac{1}{6}$	$\frac{1}{6}$	$\frac{1}{6}$	$\frac{1}{6}$
$\frac{1}{8}$ $\frac{1}{8}$	$\frac{1}{8}$ $\frac{1}{8}$	$\frac{1}{8}$ $\frac{1}{8}$	$\frac{1}{8}$ $\frac{1}{8}$		

In **5–8**, use the number line to compare. Write $<$, $>$, or $=$.

5. $\frac{2}{4} \bigcirc \frac{1}{2}$ **6.** $1\frac{1}{4} \bigcirc 1\frac{6}{8}$ **7.** $\frac{3}{4} \bigcirc 1\frac{3}{4}$ **8.** $\frac{2}{4} \bigcirc \frac{2}{8}$

9. Compare $\frac{3}{4}$ and $\frac{3}{6}$. Without using fraction strips or a number line, how can you tell which fraction is greater?

_____

_____

Name _____

Using Fractions

In **1–6**, compare. Write <, >, or =.

	$\frac{1}{2}$			$\frac{1}{2}$	
$\frac{1}{4}$		$\frac{1}{4}$	$\frac{1}{4}$		$\frac{1}{4}$
$\frac{1}{6}$	$\frac{1}{6}$	$\frac{1}{6}$	$\frac{1}{6}$	$\frac{1}{6}$	$\frac{1}{6}$
$\frac{1}{8}$ $\frac{1}{8}$	$\frac{1}{8}$ $\frac{1}{8}$	$\frac{1}{8}$ $\frac{1}{8}$	$\frac{1}{8}$ $\frac{1}{8}$		

1. $\frac{6}{8} \bigcirc \frac{1}{2}$ **2.** $\frac{2}{4} \bigcirc \frac{3}{6}$ **3.** $\frac{2}{8} \bigcirc \frac{2}{6}$

4. $\frac{1}{2} \bigcirc \frac{2}{6}$ **5.** $\frac{3}{4} \bigcirc \frac{3}{8}$ **6.** $\frac{1}{4} \bigcirc \frac{3}{8}$

7. Complete the number line by writing the missing fractions and mixed numbers.

8. About how much of this glass is filled?

A $\frac{1}{3}$

B $\frac{3}{4}$

C $\frac{1}{2}$

D $\frac{1}{8}$

9. Which fraction describes the part of this blanket that is white?

A $\frac{2}{3}$

B $\frac{1}{2}$

C $\frac{2}{4}$

D $\frac{2}{8}$

In **10–13**, name the fruit with the greater number of cups in the recipe at the right.

10. Apples or bananas? _____

11. Grapes or coconut? _____

12. Raisins or cherries? _____

13. Apples or pineapple? _____

Fruit Salad
1 batch

$1\frac{1}{2}$ cups apples
$1\frac{3}{4}$ cups grapes
$\frac{1}{2}$ cup raisins
$2\frac{2}{4}$ cups bananas
$\frac{3}{4}$ cup coconut
$1\frac{2}{4}$ cups cherries
$2\frac{1}{4}$ cups pineapple

14. One batch of fruit salad has equal amounts of which kinds of fruit? Explain how you decided.

_____

_____

Comparing Fractions on the Number Line

Yoko used a number line to compare $\frac{1}{4}$ and $\frac{3}{4}$.

She marked where $\frac{1}{4}$ and $\frac{3}{4}$ are on the number line.
Then she looked for the fraction that was farther to the right.
She wrote $>$ to show which fraction is greater.

$\frac{3}{4}$ $\bigcirc$ $\frac{1}{4}$

1. Mark $\frac{2}{3}$ and $\frac{1}{3}$ on the number line below.

Which fraction is greater, $\frac{2}{3}$ or $\frac{1}{3}$?
Hint: It will be farther to the right.
Write $>$ or $<$.

$\frac{2}{3}$ $\bigcirc$ $\frac{1}{3}$

2. Mark $\frac{1}{2}$ and $\frac{1}{6}$ on the number lines below.

Which fraction is greater, $\frac{1}{2}$ or $\frac{1}{6}$?
Hint: It will be farther to the right.
Write $>$ or $<$.

$\frac{1}{2}$ $\bigcirc$ $\frac{1}{6}$

3. Use Structure Simon is comparing $\frac{1}{3}$ yard and $\frac{2}{3}$ yard of rope.
Circle the two denominators.

$\frac{1}{3}$ $\bigcirc$ $\frac{2}{3}$

Since the denominators are the same, Simon can compare them on the same number line. Which number line should he use?

A

B

C

D

Comparing Fractions on the Number Line

In **1–3**, compare. Write <, >, or =.
Draw number lines to help.

1. $\frac{3}{4}$ ◯ $\frac{1}{4}$

2. $\frac{2}{3}$ ◯ $\frac{1}{3}$

3. $\frac{6}{8}$ ◯ $\frac{7}{8}$

In **4–6**, compare. Write <, >, or =.
Draw number lines to help.

4. $\frac{1}{2}$ ◯ $\frac{1}{4}$

5. $\frac{2}{3}$ ◯ $\frac{2}{4}$

6. $\frac{1}{4}$ ◯ $\frac{1}{8}$

7. Use Structure When do you need to use two number lines to compare two fractions?

　A When you compare fractions that have the same denominators.

　B When you compare fractions that have different denominators.

　C When you compare fractions that are greater than 1.

　D When you compare fractions that refer to different wholes.

8. Reason Explain how you can use a number line to show that $\frac{5}{8}$ is greater than $\frac{3}{8}$.

_____

_____

_____

Name _____

Finding Equivalent Fractions

Equivalent fractions are fractions that name the same part of a whole. Equivalent fractions have different numerators and denominators, but their values are equal.

You can find equivalent fractions by using fraction strips.

$$\frac{1}{4} = \frac{\Box}{8}$$

Find how many $\frac{1}{8}$s are equal to $\frac{1}{4}$. The denominator is 8 so use $\frac{1}{8}$ strips.

So, two $\frac{1}{8}$ strips are equal to $\frac{1}{4}$.

$$\frac{1}{4} = \frac{2}{8}$$

Another name for $\frac{1}{4}$ is $\frac{2}{8}$.

Complete each number sentence.

1.

$$\frac{1}{2} = \frac{\Box}{8}$$

2.

$$\frac{2}{3} = \frac{\Box}{6}$$

3.

$$\frac{3}{4} = \frac{\Box}{8}$$

4. Name two fractions that are equivalent to $\frac{1}{2}$.

_____

5. Reason Larry and Willa are each reading the same book. Larry has read $\frac{2}{3}$ of the book. Willa said that she has read more than Larry because she read $\frac{4}{6}$ of the book. Is Willa correct? Explain.

_____

_____

_____

Finding Equivalent Fractions

Complete each number sentence.

1.

$\frac{1}{4} = \frac{\boxed{}}{8}$

2.

$\frac{3}{4} = \frac{\boxed{}}{8}$

3.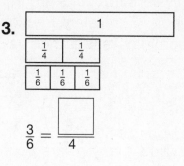

$\frac{3}{6} = \frac{\boxed{}}{4}$

Find the simplest form of each fraction.

4. $\frac{3}{6}$ _____

5. $\frac{4}{6}$ _____

6. $\frac{3}{8}$ _____

Name a fraction to solve each problem.

7. Rob colored $\frac{1}{4}$ of a rectangle. What is another way to name $\frac{1}{4}$?

_____

8. Three eighths of the cast in a musical have to sing. What fraction of the cast does not have to sing?

_____

9. Use Tools When using fraction strips, how do you know that two fractions are equivalent?

_____

_____

_____

_____

10. Samuel has read $\frac{3}{6}$ of his assignment. Judy has read $\frac{4}{8}$ of her assignment. Their assignments were the same size. Which sentence is true?

A Samuel read more than Judy.

B Judy read more than Samuel.

C They read the same amount.

D They will both finish the assignment at the same time.

Equivalent Fractions and the Number Line

Anna equally shares a bookshelf with her sister.
Her sister says Anna's books use $\frac{2}{4}$ of the shelf.
Anna thought her books used $\frac{1}{2}$ of the shelf.
Anna drew two number lines to see if the two numbers
are equivalent fractions.

The fractions are at the same location on the number line.
The fractions are equivalent. $\frac{2}{4} = \frac{1}{2}$

For **1** and **2**, use the number lines given to complete the number
sentence.

1.

$$\boxed{} \qquad \frac{2}{3}$$

$$\frac{2}{6} = \boxed{}$$

2.

$$\frac{1}{4} \qquad \frac{2}{4} \qquad \boxed{}$$

$$\frac{6}{8} = \boxed{}$$

3. Reason Mick uses two pieces of rope to make ties for two cloth sacks.
One rope is $\frac{4}{8}$ yard. The other rope is $\frac{1}{2}$ yard. He wants to know if they
are the same length. Which number line correctly models the rope lengths?

A

$\frac{1}{2}$

C

$\frac{1}{2}$

B

$\frac{1}{2}$

D

$\frac{1}{2}$

Equivalent Fractions and the Number Line

1. Write two fractions that name the location on the number line below.

For **2** and **3**, draw a number line to show that the fractions are equivalent.

2. $\frac{3}{4} = \frac{6}{8}$

3. $\frac{1}{4} = \frac{2}{8}$

4. **Reason** Explain how you can use a number line to show that $\frac{3}{6}$ and $\frac{1}{2}$ are equivalent fractions.

_____

_____

_____

_____

Whole Numbers and Fractions

Sal ate $\frac{1}{3}$ of a granola bar at breakfast. He ate another $\frac{1}{3}$ of the bar at lunch. Then he ate $\frac{1}{3}$ of the bar at dinner. How much of the granola bar did he eat in all? You can use fraction strips to model how much of the granola bar Sal ate.	Count the fraction strips. Breakfast $\frac{1}{3}$ Lunch $\frac{1}{3}$ Dinner $\frac{1}{3}$ There are three. Sal ate three $\frac{1}{3}$s of a granola bar. You can write this as the fraction $\frac{3}{3}$. Now, compare the fraction strips to 1 whole. $\begin{array}{\|c\|}\hline 1 \\\hline \frac{1}{3} \quad \frac{1}{3} \quad \frac{1}{3} \\\hline\end{array}$ So, $\frac{3}{3}$ is equal to 1 whole. You can say Sal ate $\frac{3}{3}$ of a granola bar. Or you can say Sal ate 1 granola bar.

For **1** and **2,** count the fraction strips.
Write the fraction name and equivalent whole number name for each.

1.

1			
$\frac{1}{4}$	$\frac{1}{4}$	$\frac{1}{4}$	$\frac{1}{4}$

_____

2.

1		1	
$\frac{1}{2}$	$\frac{1}{2}$	$\frac{1}{2}$	$\frac{1}{2}$

_____

For **3–6,** write an equivalent fraction for each whole number.

3. 3 _____

4. 2 _____

5. 6 _____

6. 4 _____

7. Persevere Jane gets $\frac{1}{2}$ of a gold star each time she helps her teacher clean up the classroom after art class. How many times would Jane need to help her teacher to earn 3 whole gold stars? Draw fraction strips to help.

_____

Name _____

Whole Numbers and Fractions

In **1–6**, write an equivalent fraction for each whole number.

1. 6   **2.** 8   **3.** 4   **4.** 3   **5.** 1   **6.** 5

_____   _____   _____   _____   _____   _____

7. Reason Explain how you know $\frac{6}{6}$ and 1 are equivalent.

_____

_____

_____

In **8–9**, complete each number line.

8. thirds

0     $\frac{1}{3}$ 1 $\frac{5}{3}$ 2 $\frac{8}{3}$ 3   4

9. fourths

0   1   2   3

10. Which whole number is equivalent to $\frac{8}{2}$?

  A 2   **B** 4   **C** 6   **D** 8

11. Critique Reasoning Molly is wrapping up parts of sandwiches to sell at her sandwich cart. She cuts each sandwich in fourths and then wraps each fourth separately. She says that she wrapped 16 fourths, so she wrapped 16 whole sandwiches. What was Molly's mistake?

_____

_____

_____

_____

Problem Solving:
Draw a Picture

A fence is 20 feet long. It has a post at each end. The fence also has a post every 4 feet between the two ends. How many fence posts are there in all?

Read and Understand

Step 1 What do you know?

The fence is 20 feet long.
A fence post is at each end.
There is a fence post every 4 feet.

Step 2 What are you trying to find?

How many posts the fence has

Plan and Solve

Step 3 What strategy will you use?   **Strategy:** Draw a picture

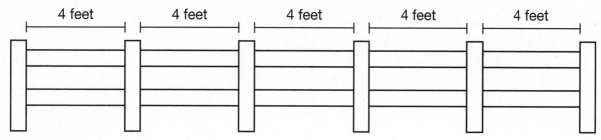

| 4 feet | 4 feet | 4 feet | 4 feet | 4 feet |

There are 6 fence posts in all.

Look Back and Check

Step 4 Is your work correct?

Yes, the picture shows a fence that is 20 feet long. It has a fence post at each end, and a fence post every 4 feet. There are 6 fence posts.

Solve. Draw a picture.

1. Jamie put 8 squares together to make a rectangle. There are 2 rows of squares. Each row has 4 squares. How many pairs of sides touch each other in the rectangle?

2. Trent, Linda, and Pam will work together to paint a poster that is 4 feet long. Each student will paint an equal length of the poster. How many feet of the poster length will each student paint?

Problem Solving:
Draw a Picture

Solve. Draw a picture.

1. Larry used a pattern of colors to make a cube train. He used a red cube, a blue cube, a red cube, and another red cube before he started the pattern again. He used 15 cubes. How many red cubes did Larry use?

   _____

2. Two pizzas were each cut into sixths. Ashraf, Drew, and Katie shared the pizzas equally. How many sixths did each friend get?

   _____

3. Eric and Frank want to equally share $\frac{4}{3}$ feet of rope. What length of rope should each friend get? Explain how to use a drawing to help solve the problem.

   _____

   _____

   _____

4. A square garden is 12 feet long on each side. Janet needs to put a post at each corner. She also needs to put a post every 3 feet on each side. How many posts does Janet need?

   A 12   **B** 16   **C** 20   **D** 24

Name _____

Classifying Shapes

You can classify polygons by finding the ways they are alike and different. Look at these two groups of polygons.

Group 1   **Group 2**

    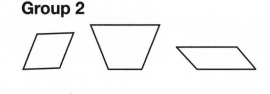

How are they similar?
All of the polygons have 4 sides and 4 vertices.

How are they different?
The polygons in Group 1 have right angles.
None of the polygons in Group 2 have right angles.

All the polygons in both groups are part of a larger group, quadrilaterals.

Use these two groups for **1–3**.

Group 1   **Group 2**

1. Tell how the shapes in Group 1 and 2 are different and how they are alike.

   _____

   _____

2. To which larger group of polygons do all of these shapes belong?

   _____

3. **Reason** Draw one more polygon that belongs in Group 1.
   Draw one more polygon that belongs in Group 2.

Classifying Shapes

For **1–2,** use the two groups below to answer the questions.

Group 1

Group 2

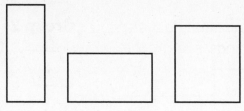

1. Tell one way the shapes in Group 1 and 2 are different and one way they are alike.

_____

_____

2. To which larger group of polygons do all of these shapes belong? _____

For **3–4,** use the two groups below to answer the questions.

Group 1

Group 2

3. Tell one way the shapes in Group 1 and 2 are different and one way they are alike.

_____

_____

4. To which larger group of polygons do all of these shapes belong? _____

5. **Writing to Explain** What characteristics help you tell the difference between a rhombus and a rectangle? Explain.

_____

_____

Name _____

Problem Solving: Make and Test Generalizations

A generalization is a statement that makes a conclusion about all of the things in a group. For example, look at these three shapes.

Make a generalization: The shapes are all acute triangles.
Test your generalization. The shape on the left has a right angle.
It is a right triangle. This generalization is not true.

Try another generalization: The shapes are all triangles.
Each of the shapes is a polygon with 3 sides. This generalization is correct.

Make and test a generalization for each set of polygons.

1.

_____

_____

2.

_____

_____

3.

_____

_____

4.

_____

_____

Name _____

Problem Solving: Make and Test Generalizations

In **1–4**, make a generalization for each set of polygons.

1.

_____

2.

_____

3.

_____

4.

_____

5. How are all of these numbers alike?

3, 5, 7, 11, 13

_____

_____

_____

6. What is the same in all of these polygons?

A They are convex.

B They are rhombuses.

C They are quadrilaterals.

D They have right angles.

7. Is this generalization true? If not, draw a picture to show why not. All triangles have at least 2 acute angles.

_____

Problem Solving: Solve a Simpler Problem

Lou sees rectangles and squares in this tile design. How many large and small rectangles and squares are there in all?

Find and count each size of square or rectangle

How many ? ⟶ 4 □

How many ? ⟶ 2

How many ? ⟶ 2

How many ? ⟶ 1 □

Add: 4 + 2 + 2 + 1 = 9   There are 9 squares and rectangles in the design.

Break the problem into simpler problems to help you solve.

1. How many rectangles in all are in the design?

_____

_____

_____

_____ rectangles in all

2. How many rhombuses in all are in the design?

_____

_____

_____

_____ rhombuses in all

Problem Solving: Solve a Simpler Problem

1. Jorge sees that there are small and large squares in the tile design below. How many squares are there in all in the design?

_____ squares in all

2. Sandi counted all the parallelograms of any size she could find in the design below. How many parallelograms are there in all?

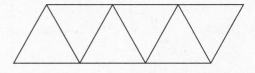

_____ parallelograms in all

For **3** and **4**, use the window design at the right.

3. Ling sees that in this window design, there are rectangles of different sizes. How many rectangles in all are in the design?

_____ rectangles in all

4. Explain the strategy you used to solve Problem 3. Draw a picture.

_____

_____

5. Eric's notebook has 30 pages. He wants to write a number on each page, starting with 1. How many digits will he write when he numbers all the pages in the notebook?

A 9　　　　　**B** 29　　　　　**C** 49　　　　　**D** 51

Name _____

Time to the Half Hour and Quarter Hour

An hour is 60 minutes long. A half hour is 30 minutes long.
A quarter hour is 15 minutes long.

The A.M. hours are the hours from 12 midnight to 12 noon.
The P.M. hours are the hours from 12 noon to 12 midnight.

The clocks show three different times.

9:30
nine thirty
half past nine

12:15
twelve fifteen
15 minutes after 12
quarter after 12

1:45
one forty-five
45 minutes after 1
15 minutes to 2
quarter to 2

Write the time shown on each clock in two ways.

1.

2.

3.

_____   _____   _____

_____   _____   _____

4. How many minutes are there in three quarters of an hour?
Explain your answer.

_____

_____

_____

Time to the Half Hour and Quarter Hour

Write the time shown on each clock in two ways.

1.

_____

_____

2.

_____

_____

3.

_____

_____

4.

_____

_____

5.

_____

_____

6.

_____

_____

7. The school bus stops at Randy's stop at 8:15 A.M. Randy arrived at the bus stop at quarter after 8. Did he miss the bus? Explain.

_____

_____

_____

8. Which does **NOT** describe the time shown on the clock?

A five forty-five

C quarter after five

B five fifteen

D fifteen minutes after five

Time to the Minute

You can skip count by fives and then count on to tell time when the minute hand is between numbers.

The minute hand is between 7 and 8.

Count by 5s from 12 to 7. That is 35 minutes.

Count 3 more minutes. There are 38 minutes.

The hour hand is between 11 and 12. The time is 11:38, or 22 minutes to 12.

Write the time shown on each clock two ways.

1.

_____

_____

2.

_____

_____

3.

_____

_____

Name _____

Time to the Minute

Write the time shown on each clock in two ways.

1.

_____

_____

2.

_____

_____

3.

_____

_____

4.

_____

_____

5.

_____

_____

6.

PM 6:23

_____

_____

7. What type of angle is formed by a clock's hands when it is 3:00? _____

8. The movie Mike watched lasted 1 hour 26 minutes. How many minutes did the movie last? _____

9. Jan's alarm clock rang at the time shown on the clock below. At what time did the alarm clock ring?

A six ten   **C** six thirty-eight

B six twenty-two   **D** seven twenty-two

Problem Solving:
Work Backward

Natalie finished listening to music at 4:30 P.M. She had listened to a
CD that lasted 40 minutes. She spent 15 minutes listening to radio
music after the CD finished. Then she listened to another CD for
45 minutes. At what time did Natalie start listening to music?

You can work backward to solve problems. Use each piece of
information to find the starting time.

Natalie finished listening to music at 4:30 P.M.

She listened to the second CD for 45 minutes.	45 minutes before 4:30 P.M. is 3:45 P.M.	
She spent 15 minutes listening to radio music.	15 minutes from 3:45 P.M. is 3:30 P.M.	
She listened to the first CD for 40 minutes.	40 minutes before 3:30 P.M. is 2:50 P.M.	

Natalie started listening to music at 2:50 P.M.

Solve the problem by drawing a picture and working backward.

1. The temperature at 6 P.M. was 72°F. This temperature was 8°F less
than at 4 P.M. The temperature at 10 A.M. was 5°F greater than the
4 P.M. temperature. What was the temperature at 10 A.M.?

_____

Problem Solving:
Work Backward

Solve the problem by drawing a picture or a number line and
working backward.

1. Will arrived at his mother's office
at 3 P.M. It took him 30 minutes to
walk from his home to the mall.
He was in the mall for 45 minutes.
It then took him 15 minutes to
walk to his mother's office. At
what time did Will leave home?

_____

2. At 12 noon, Leslie recorded
the temperature as 56°F. The
temperature had increased by 8°F
from 10 A.M. The temperature at
8 A.M. was 2°F warmer than it
was at 10 A.M. What was the
temperature at 8 A.M.?

_____

3. The test that Keyshawn's class
took finished at 10:30 A.M. The
first part of the test took 30
minutes. There was a 15-minute
break. The second part of the test
also took 30 minutes. At what time
did the test start?

_____

4. The temperature was 16°C when
Becky returned home at 6 P.M.
The temperature was 4°C warmer
at 3 P.M. than it was at 6 P.M. It
was 3°C warmer at 12 noon than
it was at 3 P.M. What was the
temperature at 12 noon?

_____

5. Elliot finished studying at 4:45 P.M. He spent 30 minutes reading a
social studies chapter. He spent 45 minutes on his math homework.
In between studying, Elliot took a 20-minute break.
At what time did Elliot begin studying?

A 3:00 P.M.   **B** 3:10 P.M.   **C** 3:30 P.M.   **D** 6:20 P.M.

Perimeter of Common Shapes

Use the properties of these common shapes to find the missing
side lengths. Then find the perimeter.

Rectangle	**Square**	**Equilateral Triangle**
Two pairs of sides have the same length.	All 4 sides have the same length.	All 3 sides have the same length.

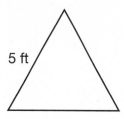

4 in. + 5 in. + 4 in. +
5 in. = 18 in.

6 cm + 6 cm + 6 cm +
6 cm = 24 cm

5 ft + 5 ft + 5 ft = 15 ft

Find the perimeter of each polygon.

1.

_____

2.

_____

3.

_____

4.

_____

5. Reason Can two squares of different sizes have the same
perimeter? Explain.

_____

_____

R 13·2

Perimeter of Common Shapes

Use an inch ruler to measure the length of the sides of each polygon. Find the perimeter.

1.

_____

2.

_____

Find the perimeter of each shape.

3.

4 m
8 m

_____

4.

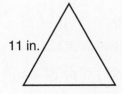

11 in.

_____

5. The largest room in Lauren's house is shaped like a square with sides of 6 yards. What is the perimeter of that room?

_____

6. The basketball court at Johnson Elementary School is in the shape of a rectangle. It is 92 feet long and 46 feet wide. What is the perimeter of the basketball court?

_____

7. A square has 9-inch sides. Every side of a pentagon is also 9 inches long. Are their perimeters the same? Explain your answer.

_____

_____

8. What is the perimeter of a hexagon that has equal sides of 12 inches?

A 60 inches   **B** 66 inches   **C** 72 inches   **D** 84 inches

Covering Regions

Area is the number of square units used to cover a region.

In the shape above, you can find the exact area by counting the number of square units that make up the rectangle.

There are 8 squares in the shape.

So, the area of the shape is 8 square units.

Sometimes you can estimate the area.

There are about 20 squares in the shape.

So, the area of the shape is about 20 square units.

Count to find the area of the shapes below.
Tell if the area is exact or an estimate.

1.

_____

_____

2.

_____

_____

3.

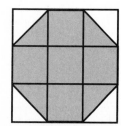

_____

_____

Covering Regions

For **1** through **4**, use the diagram below.

Athletic Field

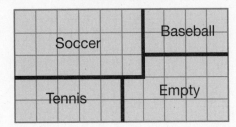

1. What is the area of the soccer section of the field? _____

2. What is the area of the field that is NOT being used? _____

3. How many square units of the field are being used?_____

4. If the school used the soccer and baseball fields to build a football stadium, how large could the area of the stadium be?

   _____

5. What is the area of the shaded section?

   A 16 square units   **B** 12 square units   **C** 8 square units   **D** 4 square units

6. What is the area of the hexagon shown below? Explain.

   _____

   _____

Area and Units

A square unit is a square with sides that are each 1 unit long.

□ = 1 square unit

The number of square units needed to cover the region inside a figure is its area.

Pam wants to make flash cards for her study group. She wants each flash card to have an area of 15 square units. Should she use square centimeters or square inches as a unit?

□ = 1 square centimeter

□ = 1 square inch

A square centimeter is a square that has a length of 1 cm on each side. If Pam uses square centimeters the area would be 15 square centimeters. That seems too small for a flash card.

A square inch is a square that has a length of 1 inch on each side. If Pam uses square inches the area would be 15 square inches. That seems a reasonable size for a flash card.

Pam should use square inches as the unit.

What is the area of each figure shown below?

1.

2.

_____

_____

3. Is the area of a paperback book cover closer to 28 square inches or 28 square centimeters? Tell how you decided.

_____

_____

_____

4. Maria wants to draw a painting with an area of 40 square inches. If she drew her painting on 1-inch grid paper how many squares would the painting cover? Tell how you know.

_____

_____

_____

Area and Units

1. Use a ruler to draw a figure with an area of 3 square centimeters.

2. Which of these figures has an area of 16 square inches?

Figure A   Figure B

☐ = 1 square inch

Figure _____

3. **Draw a Picture** Maya made a sign with an area of 48 square centimeters. Use centimeter grid paper to draw a shape that shows what her sign could look like.

4. Suppose Maya made another sign with an area of 48 square inches. Would this sign be larger or smaller than the sign with an area of 48 square centimeters? Explain how you know.

_____

_____

_____

5. What is the area of this figure in square centimeters?

☐ = 1 square centimeter

A 12   B 14   C 15   D 17

Area and the Distributive Property

Suppose you separate a rectangle into two smaller rectangles. The area of the large rectangle is equal to the sum of the areas of the two small rectangles. You can use the Distributive Property to break apart facts to find the product.

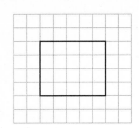

Write the multiplication fact that represents the area of the large rectangle.

$$4 \times 5 = 20$$

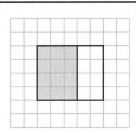

Write multiplication facts that represent the areas of each of the smaller rectangles.

$$4 \times 3 = 12 \qquad 4 \times 2 = 8$$
$$12 + 8 = 20$$

You can write an equation to show that the area of the large rectangle is equal to the sum of the areas of the two small rectangles.

$$4 \times 5 = 4 \times (3 + 2) = (4 \times 3) + (4 \times 2)$$

Write the equation that represents the picture.

1.

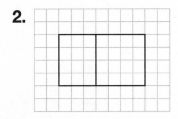

___3___ × _____ = _____ × (___2___ + _____) =

(___3___ × _____) + (_____ × ___3___)

2.

_____ × ___7___ = _____ × (_____ + ___4___) =

(_____ × ___3___) + (___4___ × _____)

Name _____

Area and the Distributive Property

Write the equation that represents the picture.

1.

_____

_____

2.

_____

_____

3.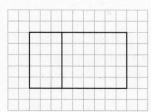

_____

_____

Choose the picture the equation represents.

4. $3 \times 9 = 3 \times (3 + 6) = (3 \times 3) + (3 \times 6)$

A

B

C

D

5. Reason Lee wants to cut this piece of canvas into two rectangles that are 3×2 and 3×5. He wants the sum of the areas of the two small rectangles to be the same as the area of the large rectangle. Can he do this? Explain.

6 feet

3 feet

_____

_____

_____

Problem Solving: Solve a Simpler Problem

How can you find the area of the shaded figure to the right?

Think of a simpler problem to solve that will help you find the answer.

☐ = 1 square inch

Find the area of the whole rectangle. $5 \times 8 = 40$

Find the area of the small rectangle. $2 \times 3 = 6$

Subtract to find the area of the shaded part.   40 sq in. − 6 sq in. = 34 sq in.

The area of the shaded figure is 34 square inches.

Solve. Use simpler problems.

1. Tyler High School has a T painted on the football field. The shaded part of the figure is the part that needs to be painted. What is the area of the painted part?

☐ = 1 square meter

2. Maria is tiling one of the walls in her kitchen. The shaded part of the figure is the part that needs to be tiled. What is the area of the part that needs tiling?

☐ = 1 square yard

_____   _____

3. **Communicate** Explain how you found your answer for Exercise 2.

_____

_____

Problem Solving: Solve a Simpler Problem

Solve. Use simpler problems.

1. Ms. Finn is going to tile her kitchen floor. The shaded part of the figure is the part that needs to be tiled. What is the area of the shaded part?

☐ = 1 square yard

_____

2. Alice is going to paint one of the walls in her bedroom. The shaded part of the figure is the part that needs to be painted. What is the area of the shaded part?

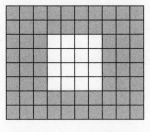

☐ = 1 square foot

_____

3. Harrison High School has an H painted on the football field. The shaded part of the figure is the part that needs to be painted. What is the area of the shaded part?

☐ = 1 square meter

_____

4. Mr. Rosen is going to repair the tiles in a shower. The shaded part of the figure is the part that needs to be tiled. What is the area of the shaded part?

☐ = 1 square foot

_____

5. Luann is going to paint an L on her fence. The shaded part of the figure is the part that needs to be painted. What is the area of the shaded part?

_____

☐ = 1 square inch

Area of Irregular Shapes

To estimate the area of an irregular shape, you can add squares on a grid, or you can subtract squares from a larger area.

Adding Squares

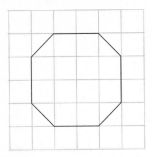

First, count the number of whole squares. There are 12 whole squares.

Then count the partial squares. There are 4 partial squares.

Estimate how many whole squares the partial squares would equal. They equal about 2 whole squares.

Finally, add the whole squares and the estimate for the partial squares to find the total estimated area.

$12 + 2 = 14$. The area is about 14 square units.

Subtract from a Larger Area

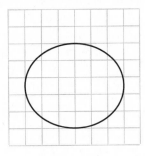

First, find the area of a regular shape that is larger than the irregular shape.

The gray rectangle has an area of 30 square units.

Subtract the squares that are not part of the irregular shape. There is about 1 square subtracted at each corner, so subtract 4 squares.

$30 - 4 = 26$. The area is about 26 square units.

Find the area of each shape.

1.

_____

2.

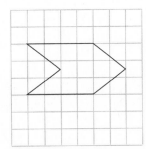

_____

Name _____

Area of Irregular Shapes

Find the area of each shape.

1.

_____

2.

_____

3.

_____

4.

_____

5.

_____

6.

_____

7.

_____

8.

_____

Same Area, Different Perimeter

Make three rectangles with an area of 18 square feet that have a different perimeter. Use grid paper or color tiles to help you.

1st Rectangle	**2nd Rectangle**	**3rd Rectangle**

Find the area:
$A = \ell \times w$
  $= 18 \times 1$
  $= 18$ square feet

Find the perimeter:
$P = (2 \times \ell) + (2 \times w)$
  $= (2 \times 18) + (2 \times 1)$
  $= 36 + 2 = 38$ feet

Find the area:
$A = \ell \times w$
  $= 6 \times 3$
  $= 18$ square feet

Find the perimeter:
$P = (2 \times \ell) + (2 \times w)$
  $= (2 \times 6) + (2 \times 3)$
  $= 12 + 6 = 18$ feet

Find the area:
$A = \ell \times w$
  $= 9 \times 2$
  $= 18$ square feet

Find the perimeter:
$P = (2 \times \ell) + (2 \times w)$
  $= (2 \times 9) + (2 \times 2)$
  $= 18 + 4 = 22$ feet

Solve.

1. Draw two different perimeters of a rectangle with an area of 14 units. Name their dimensions.

2. What is the greatest perimeter of a rectangle with an area of 39 square feet? _____

3. What is the least perimeter of a rectangle with an area of 32 square feet? _____

4. **Reason** A rectangle has an area of 42 square inches. Which has a greater perimeter, the rectangle with the dimensions 21×2 or the dimensions 6×7? _____

R 14·9

Same Area, Different Perimeter

For **1** through **9,** write "yes" if the 2 rectangles have the same area and "no" if they do not. If they have the same area, tell which one has the smaller perimeter.

1. 3   4
     8 | A | 6 | B |

_____

2. 6   10
     5 | C | 3 | D |

_____

3. 4   8
     4 | E | 2 | F |

_____

4. 5   20
     8 | G | 2 | H |

_____

5. 6   12
     8 | I | 4 | J |

_____

6. 2   3
     6 | K | 4 | L |

_____

7. 10   30
     10 | M | 3 | N |

_____

8. 4   13
     9 | O | 2 | P |

_____

9. 8   15
     8 | Q | 1 | R |

_____

10. Two rectangles have an area of 36 square inches. Name two possible perimeters for the rectangles. _____

11. The length of a rectangle is 6 inches and the width is 5 inches. Which rectangle has the same area?

A   10
     3 |_____|

B   8
     4 |____|

C   5
     7 |___|

D   20
     1 |_____|

12. Writing to Explain The area of a rectangle is 100 square inches. The perimeter of the rectangle is 40 inches. A second rectangle has the same area but a different perimeter. Is the second rectangle a square? Explain why or why not.

_____

_____

Equal Areas and Fractions

You can use equal areas to model unit fractions. Divide this square into two equal parts.

Here's one way.
Draw a line to separate the rectangle into 2 equal parts. Since each part has the same area it is $\frac{1}{2}$ of the whole.

Here's another way
Draw a line to separate the rectangle into 2 equal parts. Since each part has the same area it is $\frac{1}{2}$ of the whole.

For **1–2**, show two ways to separate the rectangle into equal parts.

1. 4 equal parts

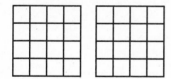

In each rectangle, what is the fraction that shows the area of one of the parts? What is the area of each part?

_____

2. 6 equal parts

In each rectangle, what is the fraction that shows the area of one of the parts? What is the area of each part?

_____

Equal Areas and Fractions

For **1** through **3**, show two ways to separate the rectangle into equal parts.

1. 4 equal parts

In each rectangle, what is the fraction that shows the area of one of the parts?

_____

2. 3 equal parts

In each rectangle, what is the fraction that shows the area of one of the parts?

_____

3. 6 equal parts

In each rectangle, what is the fraction that shows the area of one of the parts?

_____

4. Tom separated the rectangle shown below into 8 equal parts. What fraction shows the area of one of the parts?

_____

5. Mai drew the design shown below. Each square in the design has the same area. Which fraction shows the area of one of the squares?

A $\frac{1}{4}$ **B** $\frac{1}{3}$ **C** $\frac{1}{6}$ **D** $\frac{1}{8}$

Name _____

Problem Solving: Selecting Appropriate Measurement Units and Tools

When you measure the area of an object, you need to choose the best measurement unit and the best measurement tool.

Here are some measurement units that you can use to measure area.	Here are some measurement tools that you can use to measure length to find area.

square inches	square centimeters
square feet	square meters
square yards	square kilometers
square miles	

inch ruler   yardstick
or   or
centimeter ruler   meter stick

For **1** through **3,** circle the measurement unit that you would use to measure the area of each item.

1. the city of Miami

square feet
or
square miles

2. an index card

square centimeters
or
square meters

3. a TV screen

square inches
or
square miles

For **4** through **6,** circle the measurement tool that you would use to find the area of each item.

4. a postcard

inch ruler
or
yardstick

5. a classroom wall

centimeter ruler
or
meter stick

6. an ice skating rink

inch ruler
or
yardstick

7. Writing to Explain Tell which measurement tool you would use to measure the area of a student desk. Explain your thinking.

_____

_____

_____

Problem Solving: Selecting Appropriate Measurement Units and Tools

For **1** through **4**, name the measurement unit you would use to measure the area of each item.

1. blanket

2. New York City

3. table tennis table

4. vegetable garden

_____ _____ _____ _____

For **5** through **8**, name the measurement tool you would use to measure the area of each item.

5. roof of a building

6. pizza pie

7. movie screen

8. crayon box

_____ _____ _____ _____

_____ _____ _____ _____

9. Carl wants to measure the area of his kitchen floor. Which unit of measurement should he use?

   A Inches

   B Feet

   C Square inches

   D Square feet

10. Inez wants to find the area of a small photo. Which measurement tool should she use?

   A Inch ruler

   B Meter stick

   C Scale

   D Yardstick

11. Give an example of an area that you would measure in square miles.

_____

12. Jeremiah wants to use a meter stick to measure the dimensions of a magazine cover to find its area. Is that an appropriate measurement tool? Explain why or why not.

_____

_____

Name _____

Metric Units of Capacity

Two units of capacity in the metric system are milliliters (mL) and liters (L).

1 liter = 1,000 milliliters

Milliliters are used to measure very small amounts of liquid.

1 teaspoon is about 5 milliliters.

A liter is slightly larger than a quart. Many beverages are sold in 1-liter and 2-liter bottles.

Choose the better estimate for each.

1.

350 mL or 35 L

_____

2.

100 mL or 10 L

_____

3.

30 mL or 3 L

_____

4. small milk carton
250 mL or 25 L

_____

5. soup can
500 mL or 5 L

_____

6. sports cooler
4 L or 40 L

_____

7. Reasonableness Which is the better unit to use to measure the capacity of a bathtub: milliliters or liters? Explain your choice.

_____

_____

_____

Name _____

Metric Units of Capacity

Choose the better estimate for each.

1.
2 mL or 2 L

_____

2.
2 mL or 2 L

_____

3.
5 mL or 5 L

_____

4.
1 mL or 1 L

_____

5. kitchen sink
2 L or 20 L

_____

6. coffee cup
250 mL or 25 L

_____

7. thermos
2 L or 20 L

_____

8. pitcher
40 mL or 4 L

_____

Choose the better unit to measure the capacity of each.

9. tea cup
mL or L

_____

10. bath tub
mL or L

_____

11. glass of juice
mL or L

_____

12. washing machine
mL or L

_____

13. Reason A liter is equal to 100 centiliters. Is a centiliter a greater measure than a milliliter? Explain.

_____

_____

_____

14. Reason Which is the best estimate for the capacity of a large bottle of water?

A 1 L   **C** 4 L

B 400 mL   **D** 40 mL

Name _____

Measuring Capacity

A marked 1-liter container can be used to measure the capacity of other containers.

The capacity of the can is 400 milliliters.

The capacity of the bottle is 2 liters 700 milliliters.

What is the total capacity represented in each picture?

1.

_____

2.

_____

3.

_____

4.

_____

5. Use Tools Find a container that you think holds less than 1 liter. Estimate its capacity. Use a marked liter container to measure the capacity of the container you selected. Explain how your estimate compares to the actual capacity.

_____

_____

_____

Measuring Capacity

What is the total capacity represented in each picture?

1.

_____

2.

_____

3.

_____

4.

_____

5. The capacity of a small bottle of glue is 185 milliliters. How many milliliters of glue are in 5 bottles?

_____

6. Use Tools Find a container that you think holds more than 1 liter. Use a marked liter container to measure the capacity of the container you selected. Explain how you measured the capacity.

_____

_____

_____

7. Reason Benito made a small pitcher of fruit punch. He mixed together lemonade and cherry juice. Use the picture to find the amount of juice Benito made.

Lemonade   Cherry juice

A 9 liters   **C** 900 milliliters

B 100 milliliters   **D** 2 liters 900 milliliters

Name _____

Units of Mass

Mass is the measure of how much matter is in an object. Units of
mass include grams (g) and kilograms (kg).

1 kilogram = 1,000 grams

A paper clip has a mass of about
1 gram.

A large baseball bat has a mass of
about 1 kilogram.

Choose the better estimate for each.

1.

150 g or 3 kg

_____

2.

1 g or 100 g

_____

3.

300 g or 3 kg

_____

4. soccer ball
10 g or 1 kg

_____

5. tiger
30 kg or 300 kg

_____

6. dime
2 g or 2 kg

_____

7. Reason Julie has a box of paper clips that have a mass of
1 gram each. The entire box has a mass of 1 kilogram. How
many paper clips are in the box? Explain your answer.

_____

_____

_____

Name _____

Units of Mass

Choose the better estimate for each.

1.

2.

3.

4. (cookie illustration)

3 g or 3 kg	40 g or 40 kg	250 g or 25 kg	30 g or 300 g

_____ _____ _____ _____

5. crayon
20 g or 200 g

6. large dog
5 kg or 50 kg

7. quarter
5 g or 500 g

8. adult male
7 kg or 70 kg

_____ _____ _____ _____

Choose the best tool to measure each.

9. the mass of a phone _____

10. the length of a crayon _____

11. the temperature _____

12. the time for dinner _____

13. the capacity of a bowl _____

a.

b.

c.

d. (clock illustration)

e.

14. **Writing to Explain** Would you use grams or kilograms to find the mass of a letter? Explain.

_____

_____

_____

15. **Reason** Which is the best estimate for the mass of a pair of sneakers?

   A 1 kg   **B** 1 g   **C** 10 kg   **D** 10 g

Name _____

Measuring Mass

A pan balance can be used with kilogram and gram weights to measure the mass of an object.

The mass of the bunch of grapes is 1 kilogram 320 grams.

What is the total mass represented in each picture?

1.

2.

_____   _____

3. What is the mass of the cheese?

_____

4. Use Tools Find an object that you think has a mass less than 1 kilogram. Estimate its mass. Use a pan balance with kilogram and gram weights to measure the mass of the object. Explain how your estimate compares to the actual mass.

_____

_____

_____

Name _____

Practice
15-4

Measuring Mass

What is the total mass represented in each picture?

1.

2.

_____   _____

3. Reason What is the mass of one
box of nails?

_____

5. Carl bought a 340-gram package of ham. He used 85 grams
of the ham to make a sandwich. What is the mass of the
remaining package?

_____

6. The mass of a bag of grass seed is 3 kilograms. What is the
mass of 8 bags of grass seed?

_____

7. Use Tools Find an object that you think has a mass greater
than 1 kilogram. Use a pan balance with kilogram and gram
weights to measure the mass of the object. Explain how you
measured the mass.

_____

_____

_____

P 15·4

Copyright © Pearson Education, Inc., or its affiliates. All Rights Reserved. **3**

Problem Solving: Draw a Picture

Mrs. Jones bought 45 liters of juice for the school picnic. At the picnic teachers and students drank 32 liters of juice. How many liters of juice were left?

You can draw a picture of the information given in the problem to solve it.

45 liters	
32 liters	?

To find the number of liters that were left, you can subtract 45 − 32.

$$\begin{array}{r} 45 \\ -\ 32 \\ \hline 13 \end{array}$$

So, 13 liters of juice were left.

For **1-2**, draw a picture to solve.

1. Frank has a mass of 42 kilograms, and Dino has a mass of 39 kilograms. What is their total mass?

2. A small bicycle has a mass of 7 kilograms. The total mass of all the small bicycles at Mike's Bike Shop is 21 kilograms. How many small bicycles does Mike's Bike Shop have?

3. Writing to Explain How did you know which operation to use to solve Problem 2?

_____

_____

_____

Name _____

Problem Solving: Draw a Picture

The table to the right shows the mass of fat in grams per serving for certain foods. Use the table for **1–2**. Draw a picture to solve.

Total Fat (per serving)

Food	Amount of Fat (g)
Cheddar Cheese	9
Honey Ham	2
Mixed Nuts	15

1. What is the sum of the number of grams of total fat per serving for cheddar cheese and mixed nuts?

2. A package of cheddar cheese has 8 servings. How many total grams of fat are in a package of cheese?

3. The capacity of a tank of juice is 18 liters. Maggie wants to put the juice into 6 smaller containers. She wants each container to have the same amount of juice. How many liters of juice should she put in each container? Draw a picture to solve.

4. **Write a Problem** Write a real-world problem that involves mass or capacity and can be solved by drawing a picture.

_____

_____

_____

Name _____

Line Plots

A line plot is used in the same way as a tally chart. It is used to show numerical data. A line plot uses an X to show an outcome.

The data show the numbers spun in 30 spins.

Spinner Results

1	2	4	3	6	5	1	7	4	3
2	6	3	5	4	7	1	2	6	1
1	3	6	2	5	1	4	2	7	3

Sections

The line plot at the right can be used to show the data.

Number Cube Tosses

Sums

Mark played a game with two number cubes. He found the sum of the number cubes. The results are shown in the table.

1. Make a line plot to show the data.

Number Cube Tosses

Toss	Sum	Toss	Sum	Toss	Sum
1	7	11	6	21	7
2	4	12	9	22	10
3	6	13	9	23	9
4	8	14	10	24	7
5	5	15	10	25	5
6	5	16	5	26	12
7	6	17	8	27	7
8	2	18	5	28	9
9	10	19	3	29	8
10	8	20	8	30	12

2. How many Xs do you show for 8?

_____

3. Which sum from 2–12 did Mark not toss at all?

_____

Line Plots

For **1** through **4**, use the data at the right.

1. Make a line plot to show the data.

Number of Points Katie Scored

Game	Pts	Game	Pts	Game	Pts
1	23	11	25	21	24
2	25	12	30	22	26
3	30	13	27	23	25
4	25	14	22	24	28
5	21	15	26	25	27
6	26	16	21	26	26
7	21	17	29	27	29
8	24	18	25	28	30
9	28	19	21	29	22
10	20	20	23	30	24

2. How many Xs do you show for 24 points?

_____

3. Which number of points did Katie only score once?

_____

4. Which number of points did Katie score the most?

_____

5. Which two point totals did Katie score exactly four times each?

_____

For **6** and **7**, use the line plot at the right.

6. How many fewer students read 5 books than 8 books?

_____

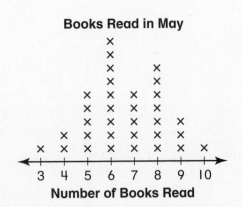

Books Read in May

Number of Books Read

7. How many students read fewer than 7 books?

A 11   **C** 17

B 14   **D** 22

Length and Line Plots

Dorothy measured the lengths of the fingers on her left hand. She also measured the length of her thumb.

Dorothy wants to make a line plot to show the measurements. The line plot can organize the data of her finger and thumb measurements.

Remember the steps for making a line plot.

Draw a number line and choose a scale based on the data collected. The scale should show data values from the least to greatest.

Write a title for the line plot.

Mark an X for each length.

1. What numbers should Dorothy use as the scale of the line plot?

   _____

2. How many Xs, or data points, should Dorothy have on the line plot?

   _____

3. Complete this line plot to show Dorothy's data.

   The Lengths of Dorothy's Fingers in Inches

   Inches

4. How long is Dorothy's shortest finger?

   _____

5. How long is her longest finger?

   _____

6. **Use Tools** Which length is used more than once?

   _____

Length and Line Plots

Japera measured the lengths of the books in the top shelf of her bookcase. She made a line plot to show the data.

Lengths of Books on Top Shelf in Inches

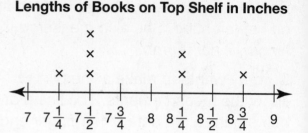

1. How many books are on the top shelf?

   _____

2. What length of book is shown most often?

   _____

She measured the lengths of the books on the bottom shelf and listed their lengths.

$8\frac{3}{4}$ in. , $9\frac{1}{2}$ in. , $8\frac{1}{4}$ in. , $9\frac{1}{4}$ in. , 10 in., $9\frac{1}{4}$ in. , $8\frac{1}{2}$ in.

3. Make a line plot that displays the lengths of the books on the bottom shelf.

   _____

4. **Use Tools** Which shelf has the most books that are the same size?

   _____

5. How many different lengths of books are on the bottom shelf?

   _____

6. **Writing to Explain** Does Japera keep the longer books on the top or the bottom shelf? How do you know?

   _____

   _____

   _____

7. Which length of book is most common on the bottom shelf?

   A 2 inches   **C** $9\frac{1}{4}$ inches

   B $8\frac{3}{4}$ inches   **D** 10 inches

Reading Pictographs and Bar Graphs

Pictographs use pictures or parts of pictures to represent data.

Gold Medals Won at 1998 Winter Olympics

Japan	🏅 🏅 🏅 🏅 🏅
Italy	🏅 🏅
Canada	🏅 🏅 🏅 🏅 🏅 🏅
Korea	🏅 🏅 🏅

Each 🏅 = 1 gold medal.

Look at the key to see what each symbol represents. Count the symbols next to a country to see how many medals were won.

Which country has the fewest symbols? Italy. How many gold medals did Italy win? 2 gold medals.

Bar graphs use bars set along a scale to represent data.

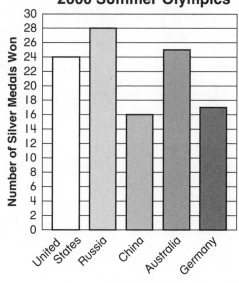

Silver Medals Won at 2000 Summer Olympics

Choose a country and use the scale to find how high the bar reaches. That number represents how many medals were won.

Which country has the tallest bar? Russia. How many silver medals did Russia win? 28 silver medals.

Use the pictograph to answer **1** and **2**.

1. How many houses were built in City B in 2002?

   _____

2. How many houses were built in City A in 2002?

   _____

Number of Houses Built in 2002

City A	🏠 🏠 🏠 🏠 🏠
City B	🏠 🏠 🏠 🏠
City C	🏠 🏠 🏠 🏠
City D	🏠 🏠 🏠 🏠 🏠 🏠 🏠

Each 🏠 = 10 houses.

Each 🏠 = 5 houses.

Name _____

Reading Pictographs and Bar Graphs

For **1** through **4**, use the pictograph at the right.

Books Read

Nancy	
Tamika	
Jamal	
Phil	

Each ▯▯ = 4 books   Each ▯ = 2 books

1. Who read the most books?

_____

2. Who read exactly 18 books?

_____

3. How many more books did Nancy read than Jamal?

_____

4. Who read the fewest books?

_____

For **5** through **8**, use the bar graph at the right.

Favorite Sport

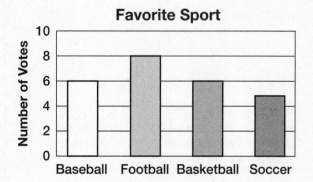

5. How many people chose soccer as their favorite sport?

_____

6. Which sport was voted as a favorite the most?

_____

7. **Reasonableness** Casey said that 40 people were surveyed. Is his answer reasonable? Explain.

_____

_____

_____

8. Which sentence is true?

A Baseball and basketball received the same number of votes.

B More people chose soccer than baseball.

C More people chose football than basketball and soccer combined.

D More people chose baseball than football.

P 16·3

Making Pictographs

The tally table shows food items that were ordered for lunch.
Follow the steps below to make the pictograph.

Food	Tally	Number
Pasta	ЖΙ	6
Salad	ΙΙΙΙ	4
Casserole	Ж Ж	10
Fish	Ж ΙΙΙ	8

Items Ordered

Pasta	🍴 🍴 🍴
Salad	🍴 🍴
Casserole	🍴 🍴 🍴 🍴 🍴
Fish	🍴 🍴 🍴 🍴

Each 🍴 = 2 meals

Step 1

Write a title that explains what the pictograph shows.

Step 2

Choose a symbol. For this pictograph, use a fork. Decide how many meals each fork will represent.

Step 3

Draw the number of symbols that are needed for each food.

The tally table shows how Ms. Hashimoto's class voted for their favorite types of movies to rent.

1. Complete the table.

Favorite Video	Tally	Number
Action	Ж ΙΙΙ	
Comedy	ΙΙΙ	
Drama	Ж Ι	
Animated	Ж Ж	

2. Complete the pictograph.

Action	
Comedy	
Drama	
Animated	

Each 📼 = ____ votes.

3. **Writing to Explain** How did you choose the number that each symbol represents?

_____

_____

Making Pictographs

For **1** and **2**, use the chart.

1. Make a pictograph to show the data in the chart. Write a title. Choose the key.

Color of Cars

Color	Tally	Number
Red	卌 卌 卌 I	16
Green	卌 卌 卌 卌	20
Silver	卌 卌 卌 卌 IIII	24
Black	卌 卌 IIII	14

2. **Reasonableness** Why did you choose the number for each symbol that you chose?

   _____

   _____

   _____

3. Fred is going to make a pictograph showing the number of tomatoes that he picked each day. He picked 30 Monday, 25 Tuesday, 35 Wednesday, and 40 Thursday. Which would be the best number to use for each symbol?

   A 1   **C** 5

   B 2   **D** 20

4. **Explain It** Pamela made a pictograph showing students' favorite drinks. Pamela drew 3 glasses to represent the 6 students who chose chocolate milk. Is her pictograph correct? Explain.

Favorite Drinks

Drink	Number of Students
Chocolate milk	⊔ ⊔ ⊔
Fruit juice	⊔ ⊔ ⊔ ⊔

Key Each ⊔ = 2 students.

_____

_____

Making Bar Graphs

The table shows the number of birds that visited a bird feeder.

Day	Number of Birds
Monday	6
Tuesday	4
Wednesday	7
Thursday	5
Friday	3

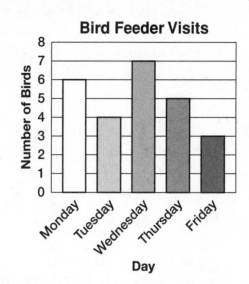

Follow the steps below to make the bar graph at the right.

Step 1	**Step 2**	**Step 3**	**Step 4**
Write each of the days and label the bottom of the graph "Day."	Number the scale. Label the scale "Number of Birds."	Make the bars for each day.	Give the graph a title.

Use the table below for **1** and **2**.

Field Day Results

Team	Points
Bulls	45
Colts	30
Pigs	25
Rams	40

1. Make a bar graph. Remember to label your graph and add a title.

2. **Writing to Explain** Why did you choose the scale you did?

_____

_____

Making Bar Graphs

For **1** and **2**, use the chart at the right.

1. Make a bar graph to show the data in the chart.

Favorite States to Visit

State	Number of Votes
New York	25
Florida	35
California	30
Hawaii	20

2. Reason How can you use a bar graph to determine which state had the least number of votes?

_____

_____

3. Explain It Describe your process for determining the scale for a bar graph.

_____

_____

_____

4. The table at the right shows the number of phone calls Mrs. Walker made during 5 days of fundraising. Which is the scale you would use to make a bar graph of the data?

Fundraising Calls

Day	Phone Calls
Saturday	26
Sunday	19
Monday	20
Tuesday	24
Wednesday	16

A by 1s

B by 2s

C by 7s

D by 10s

Problem Solving: Use Tables and Graphs to Draw Conclusions

Students were asked to name their favorite type of dog.
The pictograph shows the results of the survey.

Students' Favorite Dogs

Dog	Number Counted
Beagle	🐕 🐕 🐕
Collie	🐕 🐕 🐕 🐕 🐕
Shepherd	🐕 🐕 🐕
Poodle	🐕
Dalmatian	🐕 🐕

Each 🐕 = 2 votes.

Which dog was chosen by *exactly* 5 students? Shepherd

Which dog was chosen by 2 more students than a Dalmatian? Beagle

For **1** through **3**, use the chart below.

1. The chart shows how many points a
   football team scored. How many points
   were scored altogether?

   _____

Quarter	Points Scored
1st	7
2nd	3
3rd	10
4th	6

2. **Write a Problem** Write a word problem that
   is different from Exercise 1 that can be solved
   by reading the chart.

   _____

   _____

3. Make a graph to represent the data in the chart.
   Choose a bar graph or a pictograph.

Problem Solving: Use Tables and Graphs to Draw Conclusions

Use the pictographs for **1 through 4**.

Girls Shoes Sold at Just Shoes

Sneakers	
Sandals	
Pumps	
Boots	

Each 👞 = 10 shoes.

Girls Shoes Sold at All Shoes

Sneakers	
Sandals	
Pumps	
Boots	

Each 👞 = 5 shoes.

1. Which type of shoe was sold the most at Just Shoes?

_____

2. Which two types of shoes were sold equally at All Shoes?

_____

3. Which store sold the most pumps?

_____

4. How many sneakers were sold in all?

_____

For **5** and **6**, use the bar graph at the right.

5. How many cars were washed altogether?

_____

6. **Write a Problem** Write a word problem different from Exercise 5 that can be solved by reading the graph.

_____

_____

Cars Washed by Grade

Grade: 6th, 5th, 4th, 3rd
0 2 4 6 8 10 12 14 16 18

Students Receiving an A or a B

Test	Tally
1	卌 卌 II
2	卌 卌 卌 I
3	卌 卌 卌
4	卌 III

7. According to the tally chart, how many more students received an A or a B in Test 2 than in Test 4?

_____

Name _____

Arrays and Multiplying by 10 and 100

You can use addition to help you multiply.

Find 2 × 10.

There are two groups of 10.

Add 10 two times.
10 + 10 = 20
       or
Multiply 2 groups of 10.
2 × 10 = 20

Find 2 × 100.

There are two groups of 100.

Add 100 two times.
100 + 100 = 200
        or
Multiply 2 groups of 100.
2 × 100 = 200

Find each product.

1. Find 4 × 10.

Add: 10 + 10 + 10 + 10 = _____

So, 4 × 10 = _____.

2. Find 3 × 100.

Add: 100 + 100 + 100 = _____

So, 3 × 100 = _____.

3. Reasonableness Michael used addition to find 8 × 100 and he said the product is 80. What did he do wrong?

_____

4. Draw two sets of arrays to represent 6 × 10 and 5 × 100. Then show how to use addition and multiplication to find each product.

Name _____

Arrays and Multiplying by 10 and 100

Find each product.

1. $4 \times 10 =$ _____

2. $2 \times 100 =$ _____

3. $2 \times 10 =$ _____

4. $6 \times 10 =$ _____

5. $3 \times 100 =$ _____

6. $4 \times 100 =$ _____

7. Reason What whole number could you use to complete
☐ $\times 100 =$ ☐00 so that ☐00 is greater than 500 but less than 700?

_____

8. Mr. Mitchell does 100 sit-ups every morning. How many sit-ups will he do in 9 days?

A 90   **B** 100   **C** 109   **D** 900

9. Jackie has 10 groups of pennies with 3 pennies in each group. Carlos has 5 groups of pennies with 100 pennies in each group. Who has more pennies? Explain how you know.

_____

_____

_____

_____

Name _____

Breaking Apart Arrays

You can use arrays of place-value blocks to multiply.

Find the product for 4 × 16.

What You Show

4 × 10 = 40   4 × 6 = 24

40 + 24 = 64

Use the array to find the partial products and the product.

1.

$$\begin{array}{r} 12 \\ \times\ \ 3 \\ \hline \end{array}$$

2.

$$\begin{array}{r} 22 \\ \times\ \ 6 \\ \hline \end{array}$$

Complete the calculation.

3.
$$\begin{array}{r} 15 \\ \times\ \ 4 \\ \hline \end{array}$$

4.
$$\begin{array}{r} 22 \\ \times\ \ 4 \\ \hline \end{array}$$

5.
$$\begin{array}{r} 14 \\ \times\ \ 6 \\ \hline \end{array}$$

6.
$$\begin{array}{r} 16 \\ \times\ \ 6 \\ \hline \end{array}$$

7.
$$\begin{array}{r} 12 \\ \times\ \ 5 \\ \hline \end{array}$$

8.
$$\begin{array}{r} 13 \\ \times\ \ 4 \\ \hline \end{array}$$

9.
$$\begin{array}{r} 15 \\ \times\ \ 5 \\ \hline \end{array}$$

10.
$$\begin{array}{r} 16 \\ \times\ \ 7 \\ \hline \end{array}$$

11. Reason What two simpler problems can you use to find 4 × 22?
(Hint: Think about tens and ones.)

_____

_____

Name _____

Breaking Apart Arrays

Use the array to find the partial products and the product.

Complete the calculation.

1.
14
× 4

+

2.
12
× 5

+

3.
17
× 4

+

4.
25
× 3

+

5.
21
× 4

+

6. 4 × 17 = _____

7. 5 × 24 = _____

8. 3 × 18 = _____

9. 5 × 29 = _____

10. 23 × 3 = _____

11. 21 × 6 = _____

12. Clyde planted 4 rows of tomato seeds. Each row has 12 seeds. How many tomato seeds did Clyde plant? _____

13. Find 7 × 22.

    A 54   **B** 144   **C** 152   **D** 154

14. Write a description of an array of stickers using the product of 3 × 15.

_____

_____

_____

_____

Name _____

Using an Expanded Algorithm

You can use arrays of place-value blocks to multiply.

Find the product for 4 × 14.

What You Show	What You Write
4 × 10 = 40 4 × 4 = 16 40 + 16 = 56	14 X 4 16 4 X 4 ones +40 4 X 1 ten 56

Draw an array for each problem to find the partial products and the product. Complete the calculation.

1.   16
   × 4

2.   21
   × 6

3.   17
   × 6

4.   13
   × 2

5.   22
   × 5

6.   14
   × 3

7. Reason What two simpler problems can you use to find 7 × 38?
(Hint: Think about the tens and ones.)

_____

Using an Expanded Algorithm

Use the array to find the partial products. Add the partial products to find the product.

1.   42
   × 6

2.   37
   × 7

3.   21
   × 4

4.   35
   × 4

5. 8 × 14 = _____

6. 5 × 52 = _____

7. 8 × 42 = _____

8. 7 × 26 = _____

9. 4 × 62 = _____

10. 9 × 76 = _____

11. Rodney can type 62 words per minute. How many words can Rodney type in 5 minutes?   _____

12. Find 8 × 34.

   A 172   **B** 262   **C** 272   **D** 372

13. Explain how you can use an array to find partial products and the product for 6 × 36.

   _____

   _____

   _____

Multiplying 2-Digit by 1-Digit Numbers

Here is how to multiply a 2-digit number by a 1-digit number using paper and pencil.

Find 3 × 24.	What You **Think**	What You **Write**
Step 1 Multiply the ones. Regroup if necessary.	3 × 4 = 12 ones Regroup 12 ones as 1 ten 2 ones.	$\begin{array}{r} 1 \\ 24 \\ \times\ 3 \\ \hline 2 \end{array}$
Step 2 Multiply the tens. Add any extra tens.	3 × 2 tens = 6 tens 6 tens + 1 ten = 7 tens	$\begin{array}{r} 1 \\ 24 \\ \times\ 3 \\ \hline 72 \end{array}$

Is your answer reasonable?

Exact: 3 × 24 = 72

Round 24 to 20.

Estimate: 3 × 20 = 60   Since 72 is close to 60, the answer is reasonable.

Find each product. Decide if your answer is reasonable.

1. $\begin{array}{r} 33 \\ \times\ \ 3 \\ \hline \end{array}$

2. $\begin{array}{r} 17 \\ \times\ \ 5 \\ \hline \end{array}$

3. $\begin{array}{r} 24 \\ \times\ \ 7 \\ \hline \end{array}$

4. $\begin{array}{r} 48 \\ \times\ \ 6 \\ \hline \end{array}$

5. $\begin{array}{r} 62 \\ \times\ \ 8 \\ \hline \end{array}$

6. $\begin{array}{r} 36 \\ \times\ \ 6 \\ \hline \end{array}$

7. $\begin{array}{r} 88 \\ \times\ \ 5 \\ \hline \end{array}$

8. $\begin{array}{r} 52 \\ \times\ \ 9 \\ \hline \end{array}$

9. **Estimation** Use estimation to decide which has
    the greater product: 813 × 5 or 907 × 4.   _____

Name _____

Multiplying 2-Digit by 1-Digit Numbers

Find each product. Decide if your answer is reasonable.

1.
```
    1 8
  ×   4
  ─────
    7 ☐
```

2.
```
    2 4
  ×   7
  ─────
  ☐ 6 ☐
```

3.
```
    5 1
  ×   4
  ─────
  ☐ 0 ☐
```

4.
```
    49
  ×  7
```

5.
```
    48
  ×  5
```

6.
```
    53
  ×  9
```

7.
```
    29
  ×  6
```

8. 81 × 6 = _____

9. 89 × 8 = _____

10. 77 × 8 = _____

11. 94 × 5 = _____

12. Reason Kendra says that 6 × 65 = 390. Estimate to check Kendra's answer. Is she right? Explain.

_____

_____

13. A large truck uses about 18 gallons of fuel in 1 hour of work. How many gallons of fuel are needed for 7 hours of work?

_____

14. Which of the following is a reasonable estimate for 8 × 62?

A 48   **B** 480   **C** 540   **D** 660

15. Tyrone has 6 times as many marbles as his sister Pam. Pam has 34 marbles. Louis has 202 marbles. Who has more marbles, Tyrone or Louis? Explain how you found your answer.

_____

_____

Using Models to Divide

You can use models to help you solve division problems.
The models below can help you find 59 ÷ 4.
Find 59 ÷ 4.
Estimate 60 ÷ 4 = 15.

First divide the tens.		Now, change the tens into ones.		Next, divide the ones.		Write the remainder.	

First divide the tens.

$$\begin{array}{r} 1 \\ 4\overline{)59} \\ -4 \end{array}$$ 4 tens

Now, change the tens into ones.

$$\begin{array}{r} 1 \\ 4\overline{)59} \\ -4 \\ \hline 19 \end{array}$$ 4 tens
19 ones

Next, divide the ones.

$$\begin{array}{r} 14 \\ 4\overline{)59} \\ -4 \\ \hline 19 \\ -16 \\ \hline 3 \end{array}$$ 4 tens
19 ones

Write the remainder.

$$\begin{array}{r} 14\ R3 \\ 4\overline{)59} \\ -4 \\ \hline 19 \\ -16 \\ \hline 3 \end{array}$$ 4 tens
19 ones
3 ⟵ remainder

There is one tens block in each of 4 groups.

1 tens block and 9 ones blocks are equal to 19 ones blocks.

Each of the 4 groups has 1 tens block and 4 ones blocks.

There are 3 ones blocks left.
59 ÷ 4 = 14 R3

Use the models below to help you fill in the boxes.

1. 67 ÷ ⬚ = ⬚ R2

2. 85 ÷ 4 = ⬚ R ⬚

3. ⬚ ÷ 6 = ⬚ R5

4. 97 ÷ ⬚ = ⬚ R ⬚

Name _____

Using Models to Divide

Find how many are in each group and how many are left over.

1. 72 CDs in 5 organizers

_____

2. 54 stickers on 9 rolls

_____

3. 62 plants in 7 rows

_____

4. 98 chairs for 6 tables

_____

In **5** through **8**, use the model to complete each division sentence.

5. 23 ÷ ☐ = ☐ R3

6. ☐ ÷ 7 = ☐

7. ☐ ÷ ☐ = ☐ R2

8. ☐ ÷ ☐ = ☐ R ☐

9. Corey has 90 marbles. He decides to share them with his 6 friends so they can play a game. Which of the following models shows Corey sharing his marbles?

A

C

B

D

10. At Mr. Avery's farm there are 47 cows. There are 3 people who milk the cows each day. Does each person milk the same number of cows? Use a model to help you.

_____

_____

Name _____

Dividing 2-Digit by 1-Digit Numbers

Find 92 ÷ 6.

Step 1:	**Step 2:**	**Step 3:**	**Step 4:**
To decide where to place the first digit in the quotient, compare the first digit of the dividend with the divisor.	Divide the tens. Use multiplication facts and compatible numbers.	Divide the ones. Use multiplication facts and compatible numbers.	Check by multiplying and then adding the remainder.

Step 1:

To decide where to place the first digit in the quotient, compare the first digit of the dividend with the divisor.

$6\overline{)92}$

$9 > 6$, so the first digit in the quotient will go in the tens place.

Step 2:

Divide the tens. Use multiplication facts and compatible numbers.

Think: $6 \times ? = 6$
Multiply. $6 \times 1 = 6$
Write 1 in the tens place of the quotient.

$$\begin{array}{r} 1 \\ 6\overline{)9\,2} \\ -6\downarrow \\ \hline 3\,2 \end{array}$$

Subtract. $9 - 6 = 3$
Compare. $3 < 6$
Bring down the ones.

Step 3:

Divide the ones. Use multiplication facts and compatible numbers.

Think: $6 \times ?$ is about 32
Multiply. $6 \times 5 = 30$
Write 5 in the ones place of the quotient.

$$\begin{array}{r} 1\,5 \text{ R2} \\ 6\overline{)9\,2} \\ -6\downarrow \\ \hline 3\,2 \\ -3\,0 \\ \hline 2 \end{array}$$

Subtract. $32 - 30 = 2$
Compare. $2 < 6$
There are no more digits to bring down, so 2 is the remainder.

Step 4:

Check by multiplying and then adding the remainder.

$6 \times 15 = 90$
$90 + 2 = 92$

In **1** and **2** complete each division problem.

1.

2.

Find each quotient. Check your answers.

3. $4\overline{)86}$

4. $5\overline{)91}$

5. $3\overline{)76}$

Name _____

Dividing 2-Digit by 1-Digit Numbers

In **1** through **3**, complete each division problem.

1.

2.

3.

For **4** through **11**, find each quotient. Check your answers.

4. 2)89 **5.** 5)68 **6.** 4)92 **7.** 3)63

8. 6)96 **9.** 7)86 **10.** 2)92 **11.** 8)95

Mrs. Allen is planning to provide snacks for 72 fifth graders when they go on a field trip to the aquarium. Each student will receive 1 of each snack. Using the bar graph to the right, how many packages of each snack does Mrs. Allen need?

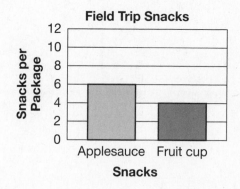

12. fruit cups _____

13. applesauce _____

14. **Reason** Which is the remainder of 37 ÷ 4?

A 1   **B** 2   **C** 3   **D** 4

15. Explain how to find the number of left over pencils if Paula wants to give 25 pencils to 6 people.

_____

_____

_____

Factors

When multiplying two numbers, you know that both numbers are factors of the product.

Example 1

Find the factors of 24.

Factors   Product

$1 \times 24 = 24$
$2 \times 12 = 24$
$3 \times 8 = 24$
$4 \times 6 = 24$
$6 \times 4 = 24$
$8 \times 3 = 24$
$12 \times 2 = 24$
$24 \times 1 = 24$

Factors of 24:
1, 2, 3, 4, 6, 8, 12, and 24

Example 2

Find the factors of 16.

$1 \times 16 = 16$
$2 \times 8 = 16$
$4 \times 4 = 16$
$8 \times 2 = 16$
$16 \times 1 = 16$

Factors of 16:
1, 2, 4, 8, and 16

List all the factors of each number. Use counters to help.

1. 16

2. 21

3. 13

_____

_____

_____

4. 25

5. 3

6. 18

_____

_____

_____

7. Reason Look at 2×7 and 3×6. Are these numbers all factors of 18? Explain your answer.

_____

_____

Factors

For **1** through **12**, find all the factors of each number.

1. 28

_____

_____

2. 19

_____

_____

3. 8

_____

_____

4. 37

_____

_____

5. 25

_____

_____

6. 11

_____

_____

7. 36

_____

_____

8. 73

_____

_____

9. 15

_____

_____

10. 17

_____

_____

11. 7

_____

_____

12. 21

_____

_____

13. Tina buys 36 party favors to give out at a picnic. Which number will NOT let her divide the party favors evenly among the guests?

A 4   **B** 6   **C** 8   **D** 9

14. Mrs. Quinn wants to arrange her students' artwork in an array on the wall. If Mrs. Quinn has 21 pictures to hang, describe the arrays she can make.

_____

_____

15. Mrs. Barry has 27 watches on display at her store. Mr. Barry says that she can make only 1 row with all 27 watches. Is Mr. Barry right? Explain.

_____

_____

_____

Modeling Addition of Fractions

Eight friends want to see a movie. Four of them want to see a comedy. Two want to see an action movie and two want to see a science-fiction movie. What fraction of the group wants to see either a comedy or a science-fiction movie?

You can use a model to add fractions.

Look at the circle. It is divided into eighths, because there are eight people in the group. Each person represents $\frac{1}{8}$ of the group. Four people want to see a comedy. Shade in four of the sections to represent $\frac{4}{8}$. Two people want to see a science-fiction movie. Shade in two more sections to represent $\frac{2}{8}$. Count the number of shaded sections. There are six. So, $\frac{6}{8}$ of the group wants to see either a comedy or a science fiction movie.

$\frac{4}{8} + \frac{2}{8} = \frac{6}{8}$ Write the sum in simplest form. $\frac{6 \div 2}{8 \div 2} = \frac{3}{4}$

Find each sum. Simplify, if possible.

1. $\frac{3}{5} + \frac{1}{5}$ _____

2. $\frac{4}{6} + \frac{2}{6}$ _____

3. $\frac{3}{8} + \frac{3}{8}$ _____

4. $\frac{2}{6} + \frac{1}{6}$ _____

5. $\frac{2}{5} + \frac{2}{5}$ _____

6. $\frac{4}{10} + \frac{6}{10}$ _____

7. $\frac{5}{8} + \frac{3}{8}$ _____

8. $\frac{4}{10} + \frac{1}{10}$ _____

9. $\frac{3}{4} + \frac{1}{4}$ _____

10. $\frac{3}{10} + \frac{6}{10}$ _____

11. $\frac{2}{6} + \frac{1}{6} + \frac{2}{6}$ _____

12. $\frac{1}{12} + \frac{4}{12} + \frac{3}{12}$ _____

13. **Reason** We can express time as a fraction of an hour. For example, 15 minutes is $\frac{1}{4}$ hour. 30 minutes is $\frac{1}{2}$ hour. What fraction of an hour is 45 minutes?

_____

Modeling Addition of Fractions

Find each sum. Simplify if possible. You may use fraction strips.

1. $\frac{2}{4} + \frac{1}{4}$ _____

2. $\frac{1}{5} + \frac{1}{5}$ _____

3. $\frac{3}{12} + \frac{8}{12}$ _____

4. $\frac{2}{6} + \frac{2}{6}$ _____

5. $\frac{1}{2} + \frac{1}{2}$ _____

6. $\frac{3}{8} + \frac{2}{8}$ _____

7. $\frac{3}{8} + \frac{4}{8}$ _____

8. $\frac{4}{10} + \frac{1}{10}$ _____

9. $\frac{1}{6} + \frac{4}{6}$ _____

10. **Model** A rectangular garden is divided into 8 equal parts. Draw a picture that shows $\frac{3}{8} + \frac{3}{8} = \frac{6}{8}$, or $\frac{3}{4}$.

11. Each day, Steven walked $\frac{1}{12}$ mile more than the previous day. The first day he walked $\frac{1}{12}$, the second day he walked $\frac{2}{12}$ mile, the third day he walked $\frac{3}{12}$ mile. On which day did the sum of his walks total at least 1 complete mile?

_____

12. Find the missing value in the equation.

$\frac{2}{12} + \frac{2}{12} + \frac{?}{12} = \frac{1}{2}$

A 1   **B** 2   **C** 3   **D** 4

13. There are five people sitting around the dinner table. Each person has $\frac{2}{10}$ of a pie on their plate. How much pie is left? Explain.

_____

_____

_____

Name _____

Modeling Subtraction of Fractions

Karla made a pizza and cut it into 10 slices. She ate four slices. What fraction of the pizza is left?

You can use a model to subtract fractions.

Karla's pizza is divided into 10 slices. One way to show this is $\frac{10}{10} = 1$ whole pizza. Karla ate four slices of the pizza. Cross out four of the slices. Count the number of slices left. There are 6 slices or $\frac{6}{10}$ of the pizza left.

$$\frac{10}{10} - \frac{4}{10} = \frac{6}{10}$$

Write the answer in simplest form, if possible.

$$\frac{6 \div 2}{10 \div 2} = \frac{3}{5}$$

Use fraction strips or models to subtract. Simplify if possible.

1. $\frac{4}{5} - \frac{1}{5} =$ _____

2. $\frac{8}{10} - \frac{3}{10} =$ _____

3. $\frac{4}{4} - \frac{3}{4} =$ _____

4. $\frac{6}{10} - \frac{2}{10} =$ _____

5. $\frac{3}{6} - \frac{2}{6} =$ _____

6. $\frac{11}{12} - \frac{9}{12} =$ _____

7. $\frac{6}{6} - \frac{3}{6} =$ _____

8. $\frac{8}{8} - \frac{6}{8} =$ _____

9. $\frac{15}{16} - \frac{7}{16} =$ _____

10. $\frac{9}{12} - \frac{7}{12} =$ _____

11. $\frac{9}{10} - \frac{7}{10} =$ _____

12. $\frac{10}{12} - \frac{7}{12} =$ _____

13. Find n.

$$n - \frac{2}{6} = \frac{2}{6}$$ _____

Name _____

Modeling Subtraction of Fractions

Use fraction strips to subtract. Simplify if possible.

1. $\frac{9}{12} - \frac{5}{12}$ _____

2. $\frac{8}{12} - \frac{6}{12}$ _____

3. $\frac{2}{2} - \frac{2}{2}$ _____

4. $\frac{5}{6} - \frac{2}{6}$ _____

5. $\frac{6}{6} - \frac{5}{6}$ _____

6. $\frac{10}{10} - \frac{4}{10}$ _____

7. $\frac{7}{8} - \frac{4}{8}$ _____

8. $\frac{7}{8} - \frac{2}{8}$ _____

9. $\frac{4}{4} - \frac{3}{4}$ _____

10. $\frac{3}{5} - \frac{1}{5}$ _____

11. $\frac{3}{5} - \frac{2}{5}$ _____

12. $\frac{9}{12} - \frac{2}{12}$ _____

13. Find $\frac{13}{16} - n$ if $n = \frac{8}{16}$. _____

14. **Model** Harriet has $\frac{4}{5}$ tank of gas left in her car.
If she needs $\frac{2}{5}$ tank to go to her friend's house and another
$\frac{1}{5}$ tank to get back home, does she have enough gas?
Draw a diagram and explain your answer.

_____

_____

15. Alicia had $\frac{9}{12}$ yard of fabric. She used $\frac{6}{12}$ for a pillow. How
much fabric does she have left? Explain how you found your
answer.

_____

_____

Fractions and Decimals

Fractions with a denominator of 10, 100, or 1,000 can be written as a decimal. Tenths, hundredths, and thousandths are written as digits to the right of the decimal point.

The shaded part is $\frac{2}{10}$.

Write it as a decimal: 0.2

Word form: two tenths

The shaded part is $\frac{13}{100}$.

Write it as a decimal: 0.13

Word form: thirteen hundredths

Write a fraction and a decimal to tell how much is shaded.

1.

2.

3. How are the two shaded grids alike? How are they different?

_____

_____

_____

_____

Write each fraction as a decimal.

4. $\frac{9}{100}$

5. $\frac{275}{1,000}$

6. $\frac{3}{10}$

7. $\frac{9}{10}$

_____   _____   _____   _____

Write each decimal as a fraction.

8. 0.148

9. 0.07

10. 0.40

11. 0.76

_____   _____   _____   _____

Name _____

Fractions and Decimals

Write a fraction and a decimal to show how much is shaded.

1.

2.

3.

_____

_____

_____

Draw a model that shows each decimal.

4. 0.78

5. 0.16

6. 0.3

Write each fraction as a decimal.

7. $\frac{165}{1,000}$

8. $\frac{17}{100}$

9. $\frac{1}{100}$

10. $\frac{4}{10}$

_____

_____

_____

_____

Write each decimal as a fraction.

11. 0.03

12. 0.036

13. 0.5

14. 0.78

_____

_____

_____

_____

15. In the decimal models, how many strips equal 10 small squares?

    A 7   **B** 1   **C** 70   **D** 10

16. Explain the steps you would take to write $\frac{19}{100}$ as a decimal.

_____

_____

_____